It's another great book from CGP...

This book is perfect for AQA GCSE English Language students working at Grades 5-1 (also known as Foundation Level in other GCSE subjects).

It covers all the key skills in an easily accessible style — all backed up with annotated texts, practice questions and exam-style questions. And of course, it's all perfectly matched to the new AQA course.

As if that wasn't enough, we've also included a full set of realistic practice papers, plus an exam advice section with a detailed guide to all the questions!

CGP — still the best! ☺

Our sole aim here at CGP is to produce the highest quality books — carefully written, immaculately presented and dangerously close to being funny.

Then we work our socks off to get them out to you — at the cheapest possible prices.

CONTENTS

CONTENTS

Section Five — Reading: Use of Language

Section Six — Reading: Structure

Section Seven — Writing: Creative Texts

Section Eight — Writing: Non-Fiction Texts

Section Nine — Practice Exams

Commonly Misspelled Words

Published by CGP

Editors:
Joe Brazier
Emma Crighton
Joanna Daniels

With thanks to Claire Boulter and John Sanders for the proofreading.
With thanks to Heather Hill for the copyright research.

Acknowledgements:

AQA material is reproduced by permission of AQA.

With thanks to iStockphoto.com for permission to use the images on pages 1, 13, 28, 49, 54, 56, 65, 73, 79, 83 & 86.

Letter on page 17 to Princess (later Queen) Victoria from King Leopold I of Belgium, August 1832, from The Letters of Queen Victoria, Volume 1 (of 3), 1837-1843.

Extract from The Snow Child by Eowyn Ivey on page 84 © 2012 Eowyn Ivey. Reproduced by permission of Headline Publishing Group & Reagan Arthur Books/Little Brown and Company.

First interview on page 88 adapted from "Of the life of an orphan girl, a street-seller", London Labour and the London Poor, volume 1 by Henry Mayhew, published in the 1840s.

Second interview on page 88 adapted from "Of children sent out as street-sellers by their parents", London Labour and the London Poor, volume 1 by Henry Mayhew, published in the 1840s.

Every effort has been made to locate copyright holders and obtain permission to reproduce sources.
For those sources where it has been difficult to trace the copyright holder of the work, we would be grateful
for information. If any copyright holder would like us to make an amendment to the acknowledgements,
please notify us and we will gladly update the book at the next reprint. Thank you.

ISBN: 978 1 78294 468 3
Printed by Elanders Ltd, Newcastle upon Tyne.
Clipart from Corel®

Based on the classic CGP style created by Richard Parsons.

Exam Structure

This section is all about what you can expect to find in your exam papers.

Stuart was starting to wish
that his GCSEs were fictional.

You will sit two different exam papers

1) Paper 1 is about <u>fiction</u> (made-up writing). Paper 2 is about <u>non-fiction</u> (factual writing).

2) Both papers are split into two sections:

- <u>Section A</u> contains <u>reading</u> questions, which test your ability to <u>understand</u> and <u>analyse</u> texts.

- <u>Section B</u> contains a <u>writing</u> question, which tests your ability to write a text <u>of your own</u>.

3) Each paper is worth <u>half</u> of your GCSE.

4) You will have <u>1 hour 45 minutes</u> to complete each paper.

5) In each exam, you should spend the first <u>15 minutes</u> reading the <u>questions</u> and the <u>source texts</u>.

Paper 1 has one source to read

Have a look at pages 2-6 for more about the questions in paper 1.

1) For <u>paper 1</u>, you'll be given a <u>question paper</u> and a separate <u>source text</u>.

2) The <u>source text</u> will be a piece of <u>fiction</u> writing.

3) It will be from either the <u>20th century</u> (1900-1999) or the <u>21st century</u> (2000 onwards).

4) Here's a bit about the <u>two</u> sections in paper 1:

> <u>Section A: Reading</u> is worth <u>40 marks</u>. It has four questions.
>
> <u>Section B: Writing</u> is worth another <u>40 marks</u>. There will be a <u>choice</u> of two tasks, but you only need to do <u>one</u> of them.

Paper 2 has two different sources to read

1) For <u>paper 2</u>, you'll be given a <u>question paper</u> and a separate <u>booklet</u> containing <u>two</u> source texts.

2) The sources will both be <u>non-fiction</u> texts.

3) One source will be from the <u>19th</u> century (1800-1899). The other will be from the <u>20th</u> or <u>21st</u> century.

4) Here's a bit about the <u>two</u> sections in paper 2:

> <u>Section A: Reading</u> is worth <u>40 marks</u>. It has four questions.
>
> <u>Section B: Writing</u> is worth <u>40 marks</u>. It only has one question. You <u>don't</u> get a choice of tasks for this paper.

There's more about the questions in paper 2 on pages 7-11.

EXAM TIP

"How did you find the exam?" "It was just on the table..."

Make sure you spend the full fifteen minutes reading the sources and the questions at the beginning of each exam. Doing this carefully will make answering the questions a lot easier.

Paper 1 — Question 1

The first question on paper 1 is fairly straightforward — you just need to do a bit of fact-finding.

Question 1 asks you to find information

1) Question 1 tests the <u>first part</u> of <u>assessment objective 1</u>:

The assessment objectives are the <u>skills</u> that you're being tested on.

> **Assessment Objective 1**
>
> • <u>Pick out</u> and <u>understand</u> pieces of <u>information</u> from the text.
> • Collect and put together information from different texts.

Question 1 tests the <u>first</u> bullet point.

2) The information you pick out might be <u>explicit</u> — that's when it's <u>obviously</u> written out in the text.

3) It might also be <u>implicit</u>, which means you'll need to <u>work it out</u> from what is said in the text.

There's more about finding information on pages 32-33 of this book.

You need to find four facts for question 1

1) Paper 1, <u>question 1</u> will look like this:

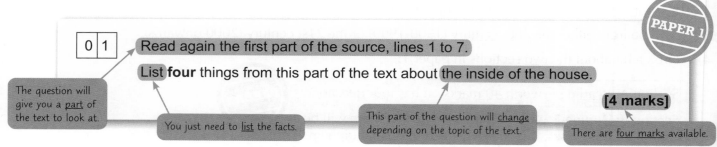

0 1 Read again the first part of the source, lines 1 to 7.

List **four** things from this part of the text about the inside of the house.

[4 marks]

The question will give you a <u>part</u> of the text to look at.

You just need to <u>list</u> the facts.

This part of the question will <u>change</u> depending on the topic of the text.

There are <u>four marks</u> available.

PAPER 1

2) You'll get <u>one mark</u> for each fact you find, so you need to find <u>four facts</u>.

3) The question will ask for facts about something <u>specific</u>. Make sure <u>all</u> your facts are about this.

4) Only write down facts from the <u>part of the text</u> that's mentioned in the question. You could draw a <u>box</u> around the section of text to help you do this.

5) You <u>only</u> need to write down <u>short examples</u>.

You can either use a short quote... ⟹ *The walls are "ocean blue".*

... or write in your own words. ⟹ *The house has blue walls.*

6) You <u>don't</u> need to write anything <u>about</u> the facts you find.

7) You should aim to spend around <u>5 minutes</u> on this question.

Paper 1 — Question 2

For question 2, you need to write about the effects of the language the writer has used.

Question 2 is about language

1) Question 2 tests assessment objective 2:

> **Assessment Objective 2**
>
> - Explain how writers use language and structure to achieve their purpose and have an effect on their readers.
> - Use technical terms to support your answer.

Question 2 tests 'language' rather than 'structure'.

2) You need to write about what effect the language has.

3) Then you need to explain how it achieves that effect.

4) You also need to use technical terms in your answer — words that are used to describe language features (e.g. metaphors, similes or adverbs) or their effects.

Have a look at section 5 for some more language features you could talk about in your answer.

Write about the methods the writer uses

1) Here's what paper 1, question 2 will look like:

You'll have to write about a particular part of the text.

PAPER 1

0 2   Look in detail at lines 11 to 20 of the source.

How does the writer use language to describe the atmosphere in the room?

You could include the writer's choice of:

- words and phrases
- language features and techniques
- sentence forms.

Write about the methods the writer uses, and their effects.

There's more on these in section 5.

Have a look at pages 44-45 for more about this.

This part of the question will change depending on the topic of the text.

This just means the length and type of sentence. There's more about this on pages 48-49.

[8 marks]

2) All your points must come from the part of the text mentioned in the question.

3) They also have to be about the topic in the question, e.g. 'the atmosphere in the room'.

4) Try to write about all of the bullet points under the question.

5) Use technical terms and plenty of examples from the text.

6) You should aim to spend about 10 minutes on this question.

You could use P.E.E.E. to write your answer to this question — see pages 12-13.

Language? Well, it's definitely written in English...

When you're writing about language, you need to talk about the effect that particular words or techniques have on the reader. Just picking out words or techniques on their own isn't enough.

Section One — The Exams

Paper 1 — Question 3

Question 3 is similar to question 2, but you need to focus on how the writer has structured the text.

Question 3 is about structure

1) Question 3 also tests assessment objective 2:

> **Assessment Objective 2**
>
> - Explain how writers use language and structure to achieve their purpose and have an effect on their readers.
> - Use technical terms to support your answer.

Jimi had never been great with structure.

2) You need to write about what effect the text's structure has.

3) Then you need to explain how it achieves that effect.

4) You need to use technical terms in your answer.

Remember, technical terms are used to describe features of a text (e.g. 'cliffhanger' or 'flashback') and their effects.

Write about a variety of structural features

1) Paper 1, question 3 will look something like this:

> *You need to write about the whole of the text.*
>
> *Think about what the overall structure of the extract is trying to achieve. E.g. an effective beginning or ending to a story.*
>
> **0 3** You now need to think about the **whole** of the **source**.
>
> This text is from the ending of a novel.
>
> How has the writer structured the text to hold the reader's attention?
>
> You could write about:
>
> - what the writer focuses your attention on at the beginning
> - how and why the writer changes this focus as the extract develops
> - any other structural features that interest you.
>
> **[8 marks]**

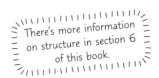
PAPER

You need to write about the writer's techniques, and the effects they have.

Try to write about all of these bullet points.

This part of the questi[on] will change depending on the topic of the tex[t]

2) You should write about the structure of the whole text, but mention the structure of paragraphs and sentences, too.

3) Use technical terms and plenty of examples from the text.

4) You should aim to spend about 10 minutes on this question.

There's more information on structure in section 6 of this book.

KEY SKILL

Con-struct-ure answers carefully...

In all of the questions apart from question 1, you should use paragraphs to organise your writing. Start a new one for each point you make. See p.14 for more about how to write in paragraphs.

Paper 1 — Question 4

Question 4 is worth 20 marks, so it's a big step up from question 3.

Question 4 asks for your opinion

1) Question 4 tests assessment objective 4:

> **Assessment Objective 4**
>
> - Evaluate a text, giving a personal opinion about how successful it is.
> - Provide detailed evidence from the text to support your opinion.

2) You need to give your opinion on how well the writer does something, such as describe a set of characters.

3) You need to support this with examples from the text, and explain how the examples support your opinion.

4) Question 4 is synoptic. This means you'll need to use everything you've learnt across the whole course to answer it properly.

Explain what you think about a statement

1) Here's what paper 1, question 4 will look like:

PAPER 1

You will only need to write about one part of the text.

| 0 | 4 | Focus this part of your answer on the second half of the source, **from line 18 to the end.**

A student, having read this section of the text said: "The writer has created a very lifelike set of characters. You feel as if you really get to know them."

To what extent do you agree?

In your response, you could:

- write about your own impressions of the characters
- evaluate how the writer has created these impressions
- support your opinions with quotations from the text.

[20 marks]

This bit will be different in your exam, but it will usually be about the techniques used and the effect they have.

You need to write about your own opinion...

...and about the methods the writer used to make you feel like this.

Give examples to back up your points.

2) In question 4, you will be given a statement.

3) You need to state your opinion — how much you agree or disagree with the statement.

4) You then need to explain why you agree or disagree, and use examples from the text to back up your points.

5) You should aim to spend around 20 minutes on this question.

EXAM TIP

It's time to get up close and personal...

To get good marks for question 4, you will need to provide a personal opinion on the source text. Don't forget to back it up with short examples, though. You need to show why it's your opinion.

Paper 1 — Question 5

Question 5 is the writing question. In paper 1, there are two tasks — you can choose which one you answer.

Question 5 tests your writing skills

1) Question 5 is a <u>creative writing</u> task. It tests <u>two</u> assessment objectives:

There's more about purpose and audience on pages 24-25.

Assessment Objective 5
- Write <u>clearly</u>, in a way that's right for the <u>purpose</u> and <u>audience</u>.
- <u>Organise</u> your writing into a clear <u>structure</u>.

Assessment Objective 6
- Use a variety of <u>sentence structures</u> and <u>vocabulary</u>.
- Write <u>accurately</u>, with good spelling, punctuation and grammar.

2) Question 5 will look something like this:

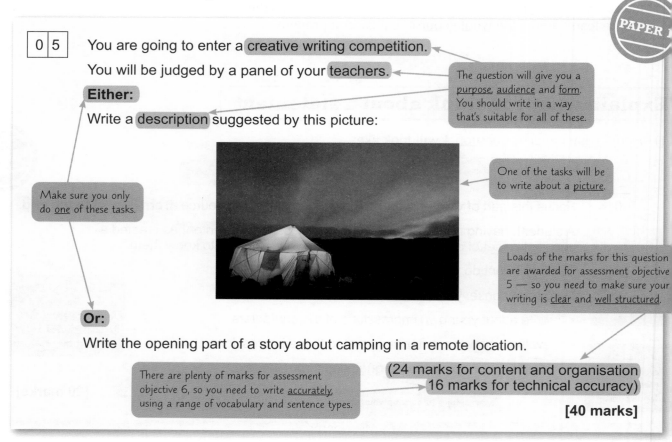

0 5   You are going to enter a creative writing competition.
You will be judged by a panel of your teachers.

Either:
Write a description suggested by this picture:

The question will give you a <u>purpose</u>, <u>audience</u> and <u>form</u>. You should write in a way that's suitable for all of these.

One of the tasks will be to write about a <u>picture</u>.

Make sure you only do <u>one</u> of these tasks.

Or:
Write the opening part of a story about camping in a remote location.

Loads of the marks for this question are awarded for assessment objective 5 — so you need to make sure your writing is <u>clear</u> and <u>well structured</u>.

There are plenty of marks for assessment objective 6, so you need to write <u>accurately</u>, using a range of vocabulary and sentence types.

(24 marks for content and organisation
16 marks for technical accuracy)

[40 marks]

PAPER 1

3) Write your answer in <u>full sentences</u>.

4) Make sure you <u>plan</u> your answer (there's more about this on p.20).

5) Spend around <u>45 minutes</u> in total on this question.

6) Give yourself 5 minutes to <u>plan</u>, 35 minutes to <u>write</u> your answer, and 5 minutes to <u>check</u> your work.

EXAM TIP

I like what you've done here. It's... err... creative...

This is your chance to show your creative side. Use lots of descriptive language and try to produce an interesting piece of writing. There's loads more information about this question in section 7.

Section One — The Exams

Paper 2 — Question 1

On to paper 2 now — that's the non-fiction paper. Here's some information about paper 2, question 1.

Question 1 is about picking out true statements

1) Paper 2, question 1 tests the first part of assessment objective 1:

> **Assessment Objective 1**
>
> • Pick out and understand pieces of information from the texts. ← Question 1 tests the first bullet point.
> • Collect and put together information from different texts.

2) The information you're looking for might be explicit — it will be obviously written out in the text.

3) It might also be implicit, so you'll need to work it out from what is said in the text.

Choose exactly four statements

1) Paper 2, question 1 asks you to pick out four true statements.

2) The exam question will look like this:

The question will give you a part of the text to look at.

PAPER 2

| 0 1 | Read again **source A**, from lines 1 to 11. |

Choose **four** statements below which are TRUE.

• Shade the boxes of the ones that you think are true

There will be 4 true statements and 4 false statements.

• Choose a maximum of four statements.

You should always select exactly four statements. If you can't pick out four that you think are true, check the text again and make an educated guess.

A	Aaron's parents think he goes to football every Thursday.	▨
B	Aaron would like to be better at sport.	☐
C	Aaron really likes board games.	☐
D	Aaron admires his brother.	☐
E	Aaron has a good relationship with his parents.	☐
F	Aaron enjoys school.	☐
G	Aaron is a high-achiever at school.	☐
H	Aaron likes living in Manchester.	☐

Shade the right answers in like this.

You'll get 1 mark for each true statement you shade in.

[4 marks]

3) Only look at the part of the text that's mentioned in the question. You could draw a box around the section of the text to help you do this.

4) You should aim to spend about 5 minutes on this question.

Some of those 'facts' are as fake as Father Christmas...

You need to show that you've understood the texts. Read the text and the statements really carefully — there might be a few false options in there that look like they could almost be true.

Section One — The Exams

Paper 2 — Question 2

Question 2 on paper 2 is all about summarising information.

You need to write about two texts in question 2

1) This question tests all of <u>assessment objective 1</u>:

> ### Assessment Objective 1
> * <u>Pick out</u> and <u>understand</u> pieces of <u>information</u> from the texts.
> * <u>Collect</u> and <u>put together</u> information from <u>different texts</u>.

Question 2 tests both bullet points.

2) You need to show that you can pick out information from <u>two texts</u> about <u>something in particular</u>.

3) You then need to <u>summarise</u> the information.

4) That means you need to use your <u>own words</u> to make key points about <u>both texts</u> and show how they are <u>similar</u> or <u>different</u>.

Pick out the similarities or differences between the sources

1) Here's how <u>question 2</u> will look in the exam:

You need to write about <u>both</u> source texts in your answer.

PAPER 2

> **0 2** You need to refer to **source A** and **source B** for this question:
>
> Use details from both sources.
> Write a summary of the differences between Jane and Mrs Silverton.
>
> **[8 marks]**

Remember to include <u>examples</u> in your answer.

The question is asking you to <u>summarise</u> information from both texts.

The question will ask about the <u>similarities</u> or <u>differences</u> between a pair of characters or on a particular topic.

2) Question 2 asks you to summarise some <u>similarities</u> or <u>differences</u> between the two texts.

3) Make sure you <u>only</u> write about the <u>topic</u> or <u>pair of characters</u> that the question asks about.

4) You need to write about <u>both</u> source texts, and include plenty of <u>examples</u> from both texts.

5) You should use <u>linking words</u> in your answer to highlight the differences or similarities between the texts.

See p.36 for more about linking words.

6) You should aim to spend about <u>8 minutes</u> on this question.

Summer-ise yourself — wear a sunhat all year round...

Summarising two things can be tricky. Concentrate on making a few solid comparisons instead of trying to pick up on every last detail. There's loads more about summarising on pages 36-37.

Paper 2 — Question 3

Paper 2, question 3 will ask you about the effects of the language used in one of the sources.

Question 3 is about the effect of the writer's language

1) This question tests <u>assessment objective 2</u>.

Assessment Objective 2

- <u>Explain</u> how writers use <u>language</u> and <u>structure</u> to achieve their <u>purpose</u> and have an <u>effect</u> on their readers.
- Use <u>technical terms</u> to support your answer.

Question 3 tests 'language' rather than 'structure'.

2) You need to write about what <u>effect</u> the <u>language</u> has.

3) Then you need to explain <u>how</u> it achieves that effect.

4) You also need to use <u>technical terms</u> in your answer — words that are used to describe <u>language features</u> or their <u>effects</u>.

No language technique was going to help Dad get Alex off to sleep.

Think about the writer's choice of words

You could use P.E.E.E. to answer this question — see pages 12-13.

1) Have a look at this <u>question</u> — it's like the one you'll get in the <u>exam</u>:

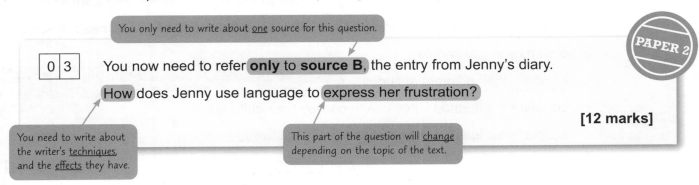

You only need to write about <u>one</u> source for this question.

| 0 | 3 | You now need to refer **only** to **source B**, the entry from Jenny's diary.

How does Jenny use language to express her frustration?

[12 marks]

PAPER 2

You need to write about the writer's <u>techniques</u>, and the <u>effects</u> they have.

This part of the question will <u>change</u> depending on the topic of the text.

2) Make sure you <u>only</u> write about the source mentioned in the question.

3) You need to explain <u>how</u> the writer uses <u>language</u> to have an <u>effect</u> on the reader.

See section 5 for more about language and its effects.

4) Be specific — write about individual <u>words and phrases</u>, <u>language techniques</u> and different <u>sentence forms</u>.

5) Support all your <u>points</u> with <u>examples</u> from the text, and use <u>technical terms</u> when you can.

6) You should aim to spend around <u>12 minutes</u> on this question.

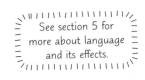

EXAM TIP

My mum always told me to watch my language...

If you spot a particular technique that's being used, make sure you name it — there are marks for knowing your technical terms in this exam. Don't forget to explain the effect that it creates, too.

Paper 2 — Question 4

Question 4 is the longest reading question in paper 2. In it, you have to compare ideas across both texts.

Question 4 asks you to make a comparison

Comparisons are where you explain how two texts are similar or different.

1) This question tests assessment objective 3:

Assessment Objective 3

- Identify different writers' ideas and viewpoints.
- Compare the methods used by different writers to convey their ideas.

2) You'll need to pick out different writers' attitudes and compare them with each other.

3) You'll also need to compare how the writers have conveyed their attitudes — the techniques that they use

4) Question 4 is synoptic. This means you'll need to use everything you've learnt across the whole course to answer it properly.

Compare the viewpoints of two writers

P.E.E.E. will be useful for this question — see pages 12-13.

1) Question 4 will look like this:

PAPER 2

You need to write about both source texts in your answer.

| 0 | 4 |

For this question, you need to refer to **the whole of source A** together with **source B**.

Compare how the two writers convey their different attitudes to dieting and healthy eating.

This part of the question will change depending on the topic of the text

In your answer, you should:

- compare their different attitudes

Write about how the writers have used language and structure to show their attitudes.

Identify and compare the writers' attitudes.

- compare the methods they use to convey their attitudes
- support your ideas with quotations from both texts.

You need to give examples from both sources.

[16 marks]

2) In question 4, you need to write about both writers' points of view.

3) You'll be given a particular topic to write about. Make sure all your points are about that topic.

4) Try to write about all the things that are mentioned in the bullet points.

5) You need to link the two texts together in your answer. After you make a point about a text, you should explain how it's similar or different to the other text.

6) You should aim to spend about 20 minutes on this question.

KEY SKILL

Just don't compare answers with the person next to you...

Comparing is an important skill. Make sure you make links between the two texts in your answer, and then explain how they're similar or different. There's more about this on pages 18-19.

Paper 2 — Question 5

Question 5 is the last question in paper 2. It's another writing question, and this time it's non-fiction.

Question 5 tests two assessment objectives

1) Question 5 tests your <u>writing skills</u>.

2) Here are the <u>assessment objectives</u> you're being tested on:

There's more about purpose and audience on pages 24-25.

Assessment Objective 5

- Write <u>clearly</u>, in a way that's right for the <u>purpose</u> and <u>audience</u>.

- <u>Organise</u> your writing into a clear <u>structure</u>.

Assessment Objective 6

- Use a variety of <u>sentence structures</u> and <u>vocabulary</u>.

- Write <u>accurately</u>, with good spelling, punctuation and grammar.

3) It's really important to write in a way that will <u>interest</u> your audience.

4) Your answer also needs to <u>achieve a purpose</u> — usually to <u>argue</u>, <u>persuade</u>, <u>advise</u>, <u>entertain</u> or <u>inform</u> the reader.

5) <u>Question 5</u> will usually look something like this:

| 0 | 5 | 'School uniforms are a pointless expense. They are never worn correctly, they are uncomfortable and they restrict pupils' creativity.'

Write a letter to your headteacher, in which you persuade them to agree with your point of view on this statement.

Lots of the marks in this question are for assessment objective 5 — so make sure your writing is <u>clear</u> and <u>well structured</u>.

...e question will ...: you to respond ...a <u>prompt</u> like ...s one. It might ...an opinion, ...ituation or a ...tement.

This part of the question will give you the <u>form</u>, <u>audience</u> and <u>purpose</u>. You should write in a way that's suitable for these.

There are also plenty of marks for assessment objective 6, so you need to write <u>accurately</u>, using a range of vocabulary and sentence types.

(24 marks for content and organisation
16 marks for technical accuracy)

[40 marks]

6) You'll need to write in the style of a <u>non-fiction text</u>, e.g. a newspaper article.

7) The question will ask you to give your <u>own viewpoint</u> on something. It will be on a similar <u>theme</u> to the sources from the <u>reading section</u>.

8) Write a short <u>plan</u> before you start (see p.20 for how to do this).

9) Write your answer in <u>full sentences</u>.

10) Spend about <u>45 minutes</u> in total on this question.

11) Give yourself 5 minutes to <u>plan</u>, 35 minutes to <u>write</u> your answer, and 5 minutes to <u>check</u> your work.

Joe's viewpoint on the issue was: 'from above'.

Your true colours need to do more than just shine through...

You need to be able to put across your opinion in a way that's really clear and obvious to the examiner. Make sure it's still interesting to read, though — that's the ticket to a top answer.

P.E.E.E.

P.E.E.E. can help you structure your answers clearly. It stands for <u>P</u>oint, <u>E</u>xample, <u>E</u>xplain, <u>E</u>ffect. You might find this structure helpful for answering paper 1, questions 2, 3 and 4 and paper 2, questions 3 and 4.

The P stands for 'Point'

1) Start each paragraph by <u>stating</u> the <u>point</u> you're going to make.

2) Each point you make needs to clearly <u>answer the question</u> you've been asked.

Question
This question is asking you about the writer's use of <u>language</u> and the feelings it creates.

0 2   How does the writer use language to show how she feels about school dinners?

The writer uses strong adjectives to show how angry she feels about school dinners.

Point
This makes a point straight away that clearly <u>answers the question</u>.

3) To structure your <u>whole answer</u>, you could write a new paragraph for each point you make, and put all the parts of P.E.E.E. into each paragraph.

The first E stands for 'Example'

You <u>always</u> need to include an <u>example</u> to back up your point.
There are <u>two ways</u> of doing this:

1) You can include a <u>short quote</u> from the text:

Remember to always put your quote inside a pair of speech marks (" ").

0 2   How does the writer use language to show how she feels about school dinners?

The writer uses strong adjectives to show how angry she feels about school dinners. She describes herself as "furious", and "incandescent" with rage.

Example
These are quotes. They repeat the exact words from the text.

2) You can also <u>paraphrase</u> from the text — that's when you describe something that's said, or one of the <u>writer's techniques</u>, in your <u>own words</u>:

0 2   How does the writer use language to show how she feels about school dinners?

The writer uses rhetorical questions to show how angry she feels about school dinners. In the third paragraph, she includes several short questions in a row.

Example
This is a paraphrase. It <u>describes</u> a feature of the text.

P.E.E.E.

The second E stands for 'Explain'

1) Examples are important, but they're not very <u>useful</u> on their own.

2) You also need to <u>explain</u> how the example <u>proves</u> the <u>point</u> you've made:

>
>
> | 0 | 2 | How does the writer use language to show how she feels about school dinners?
>
>   *The writer uses strong adjectives to show how angry she feels about school dinners. She describes herself as "furious", and "incandescent" with rage. These words evoke images of violence and destruction, which convey the idea that her anger is very strong.*

Explanation
This sentence explains <u>how</u> the example backs up the point.

The last E stands for 'Effect'

1) You can often go further by explaining the <u>effect</u> <u>on the reader</u> of your <u>example</u> or your <u>point</u>.

2) You could write about things like:

- how the text makes the reader <u>feel</u>

- how it helps the reader to <u>understand</u> something

- how it <u>persuades</u> the reader to do something.

April had always believed in leading by egg-sample.

© Tsekhmister/iStockphoto.com

>
>
> | 0 | 2 | How does the writer use language to show how she feels about school dinners?
>
>   *The writer uses strong adjectives to show how angry she feels about school dinners. She describes herself as "furious", and "incandescent" with rage. These words evoke images of violence and destruction, which convey the idea that her anger is very strong. This kind of descriptive language might remind the reader of similar feelings they have had, so they would understand the writer's emotions better.*

Effect
This talks about the <u>effect</u> that the writer's techniques have on the reader.

KEY SKILL

P.E.E.E. — when one vowel just isn't enough...

Using P.E.E.E. will really improve your answers. Make sure that you learn it, practise using it, and then practise using it some more — you'll be a P.E.E.E. expert by the time you get to your exam.

Answering Reading Questions

It's really important to write clear answers in the exams. These two pages will give you some tips on how to write your answers to the longer reading questions (that's questions 2, 3 and 4 on both papers).

Don't rush into answering the questions

1) Before you start answering any of the exam questions, you should spend about 15 minutes reading through the questions and the texts.

2) Always read the questions before the texts — that way, you'll know what to look out for.

3) To help you work out what the questions are asking you to do, underline any key words:

> | 0 | 2 | Write a summary of the differences between the two main characters.

4) Once you've read the questions, carefully read through the texts.

5) It's a good idea to underline key words or phrases that will help you to answer the questions — but don't spend ages doing this.

Remember, it's your exam paper — you can write on it if it helps you.

6) You don't need to write a plan for most of the reading questions, but for question 4 on each paper you might want to jot down a short plan before you start writing your answer.

Use paragraphs to structure your answer

There's some info on pages 12-13 on how to use P.E.E.E. in your paragraphs.

1) To organise your answers clearly, you need to write in paragraphs.

2) Start a new paragraph for each new point you make.

3) Show that it's a new paragraph by starting a new line and leaving a gap, like this:

> *... The writer is alone: he says that he "only had one sister, long dead now". This implies that he has no other family, so the reader feels sorry for the writer.*
> *However, the writer can also be cruel. He calls Nina "unrefined", suggesting that he doesn't respect her. This makes the reader lose sympathy for the writer...*

4) Link your paragraphs together to make your writing more organised and clear.

5) Use linking words and phrases like these to help you:

| However... | In contrast... | On the other hand... | Equally... |
| In the same way... | In addition... | Alternatively... | Conversely... |

Try to use lots of different linking words — don't just repeat the same ones again and again.

Answering Reading Questions

Don't make your sentences too long

1) Make sure your sentences aren't too <u>long</u> and <u>confusing</u> to read.

2) Instead of writing one long sentence, try <u>splitting</u> it into <u>a few shorter sentences</u>.

3) You can use <u>explaining</u> words and phrases to make sure that your sentences still <u>link together</u>, for example:

| This suggests that... | This highlights the fact that... | This emphasises... |

| Furthermore... | This continues the idea of... |

4) Too many <u>very</u> short sentences can be <u>difficult to read</u> though, so try to use a <u>mix</u> of different sentence lengths.

Use the right vocabulary to get your point across

Formal language is sometimes called Standard English.

1) You need to use <u>formal language</u> when answering the reading questions.

2) Don't use any <u>slang</u> or <u>informal</u> words that your examiner <u>might not understand</u>.

3) Avoid using <u>contractions</u> — <u>shortened words</u> such as 'don't' and 'isn't'.

4) Don't be too <u>vague</u>:

The brothers seem a bit weird. This isn't <u>specific</u> enough — you need to say <u>what</u> it is that's 'weird' about the characters.

The brothers react rudely to Tia, despite the fact that she is always very kind to them. This is much <u>better</u> — it explains <u>exactly</u> what's weird about the brothers.

5) Try to make your writing sound <u>interesting</u>. Don't just stick to the <u>same</u> words all the time:

The writer makes the forest sound really nice. The colours are nice so it sounds like it would be nice to be there. This uses the word 'nice' three times, which is very <u>repetitive</u>.

The writer makes the forest sound very appealing. The colours are really vivid, which makes the reader want to visit the forest. ⟹ This uses lots of <u>different</u> words, such as '<u>appealing</u>' and '<u>vivid</u>', to really get the point across.

6) Avoid using <u>clichés</u> (words and phrases that are so commonly used that they've lost their effect) like 'at the end of the day'.

KEY SKILL

At the end of the day, your answer needs to make sense...

You might have something brilliantly interesting to say, but if the examiner can't understand your point, then you won't get credit for it. That's why it's so important to nail these writing skills.

19th-Century Texts

In paper 2, you'll always be given a 19th-century non-fiction text to write about — that's a text that was written between 1800 and 1899. These two pages will give you some help with reading this type of text.

19th-century texts are a bit different to modern texts

1) 19th-century texts often sound more <u>formal</u> than modern writing.

2) You might not <u>recognise</u> some of the words — but any words that aren't used today will be defined in a <u>glossary</u> at the end of the source.

If you find a sentence hard to understand, try re-reading it, and think about what the text around it says.

3) The sentences can be <u>quite long</u> and the <u>word order</u> can sometimes be different to modern texts. Here are some examples:

Then, Albert being gone and we two left alone, Edward enquired as to whether I might accompany him on a stroll in the garden.

- The language is <u>formal</u>. For example, it uses 'enquired' instead of 'asked'.
- 'Albert being gone and we two left alone' is just <u>another way</u> of saying 'Albert had gone and the two of us were left alone.'

I believe it necessary to abandon this foul enterprise.

Sometimes it can seem as if a word has been <u>missed out</u>. Today we might put an '<u>is</u>' after '<u>it</u>' in this sentence.

Maude had spent many thrilling hours thinking about word order.

19th-century society was different to today

Knowing about 19th-century <u>society</u> will help you to understand the <u>text</u> better in the exam.

Social Class

- Early 19th-century society was <u>divided</u> between the rich <u>upper classes</u> (who owned the land) and the poorer <u>working classes</u>.
- During the 19th century, the <u>Industrial Revolution</u> created opportunities for more people to make more <u>money</u>.

Education

- In the <u>early</u> 19th century, <u>not many</u> children went to school.
- Children from <u>poor families</u> often <u>worked</u> to help support their families instead.
- <u>Rich</u> families often sent their children to <u>boarding school</u>, or hired a <u>governess</u> to teach them at <u>home</u>.

Women

- Most women were expected to be in charge of looking after their <u>home</u> and <u>children</u>.
- Women didn't have as many <u>rights</u> as men — they couldn't <u>vote</u> in elections, and they often didn't <u>control</u> their own money.

Religion

- Most middle- and upper-class people attended <u>church</u> regularly.
- However, <u>science</u> was starting to challenge some religious ideas.

19th-Century Texts

Have a look at this piece of 19th-century writing

This is a letter written to Princess (later Queen) Victoria of the United Kingdom by her uncle, King Leopold I of Belgium. In it, Leopold describes his new wife, Louise Marie.

Laeken, 31st August 1832.

MY DEAREST LOVE,—You told me you wished to have a description of your new Aunt. I therefore shall both mentally and physically describe her to you.

She is extremely gentle and amiable, her actions are always guided by principles. She is at all times ready and disposed to sacrifice her comfort and inclinations to see others happy. She values goodness, merit, and virtue much more than beauty, riches, and amusements. With all this she is highly informed and very clever; she speaks and writes English, German and Italian; she speaks English very well indeed. In short, my dear Love, you see that I may well recommend her as an example for all young ladies, being Princesses or not.

Now to her appearance. She is about Feodore's* height, her hair very fair, light blue eyes, of a very gentle, intelligent and kind expression. A Bourbon** nose and small mouth. The figure is much like Feodore's but rather less stout. She rides very well, which she proved to my great alarm the other day, by keeping her seat though a horse of mine ran away with her full speed for at least half a mile. What she does particularly well is dancing. Music unfortunately she is not very fond of, though she plays on the harp; I believe there is some idleness in the case. There exists already great confidence and affection between us; she is desirous of doing everything that can contribute to my happiness, and I study whatever can make her happy and contented.

You will see by these descriptions that though my good little wife is not the tallest Queen, she is a very great prize which I highly value and cherish...

Now it is time I should finish my letter. Say everything that is kind to good Lehzen***, and believe me ever, my dearest Love, your faithful Friend and Uncle,

LEOPOLD R.

Glossary

* Feodore — Victoria's half-sister, Princess Feodora

** Bourbon — the Bourbons were the French royal family

*** Lehzen — Princess Victoria's governess, Louise Lehzen

Tone
The tone is affectionate but the language is still formal.

19th-century society
'Virtue' was an important quality — it means having strong morals.

19th-century society
Upper-class women were often expected to learn certain skills, such as riding, dancing and playing music.

Writing style
19th-century texts often phrase things differently. A modern writer might have said "I should end this letter here."

19th-century society
Upper-class women were educated in European languages.

19th-century society
This text gives us an idea of what was valued in upper-class women.

Writing style
If you come across a tricky sentence, use the rest of the text to work out what's going on. Here, Leopold is saying that Louise Marie doesn't try very hard at playing the harp.

19th-century society
Women were often seen as belonging to their husbands.

Writing style
Superlatives (words that describe the most or biggest something can be) are common in 19th-century writing.

19th-century texts — unlikely to contain any emojis...

It's important to be able to read and understand 19th-century texts. This stuff might look a bit like History rather than English, but it'll really help you to improve some of your answers in the exam.

Comparing Texts

In paper 2, you'll be given two texts. For questions 2 and 4, you'll need to make comparisons between them.

Comparing is all about looking at two things together

1) Comparing means finding <u>similarities</u> and <u>differences</u>.

2) The exam questions will tell you <u>what</u> to compare between the two texts.

3) It might be two <u>characters</u>, a <u>topic</u> that the texts have in common, or the <u>writers' viewpoints</u> on something.

Some questions might not use the word 'compare'. However, if it's asking you about more than one text, it's always a compare question.

4) To help you answer comparing questions, you could <u>underline</u> relevant parts of the text as you <u>read</u>. For example:

If you were asked to <u>compare</u> the two types of <u>bear</u> in these texts, you might <u>underline</u> these bits:

Source A
The <u>Arctic-dwelling</u> polar bear's white fur acts as the perfect camouflage, making it a <u>formidable</u> <u>hunter</u> of <u>seals</u>, which are its <u>main food source</u>.

Source B
Grizzly bears are <u>omnivorous</u> animals — they commonly eat <u>nuts, berries and leaves</u> as well as the animals that they <u>hunt</u> in their <u>North American habitat</u>.

5) You can then use the bits you've underlined to help write the <u>points</u> and <u>examples</u> for your answer.

6) For question 4, you could also use the underlined bits to make a short <u>plan</u>.

Write about the links between the two texts

1) To <u>structure</u> your comparison, you could write a <u>whole paragraph</u> about one text, then a paragraph about the <u>other</u>.

2) Or you could make comparative points about <u>both texts</u> within a paragraph.

3) However you structure your points, you need to use <u>linking words and phrases</u> to make your comparisons clear. For example:

<u>In contrast</u>, the habitat of the polar bear is confined to the Arctic region. This could mean that polar bears are more threatened by climate change than grizzly bears.

This paragraph starts with a <u>linking</u> <u>phrase</u> ('In contrast'), to make it clear that it's introducing a <u>comparison</u> with the previous paragraph.

Polar bears are primarily carnivorous, as seals are their "main food source". Grizzly bears, <u>however</u>, "commonly" eat plants as well as animals. Having a more varied diet might mean that grizzly bears are more adaptable than polar bears.

This uses the word '<u>however</u>' to link together two points about <u>different</u> <u>texts</u> in the <u>same paragraph</u>.

Have a look at p.14 for some more linking words and phrases.

Comparing Texts

Make your comparisons structured and clear

1) Here are some <u>tips</u> to keep in mind when you're comparing texts:

- Use <u>linking words and phrases</u> to make <u>clear</u> comparisons.
- Make sure your comparisons are about the <u>pair of characters</u>, <u>topic</u> or <u>writers' viewpoints</u> that are mentioned in the question.
- Use plenty of examples from <u>both sources</u> to back up your points.
- Make sure you <u>structure</u> your answer clearly, e.g. by using <u>paragraphs</u>.

Marvin's viewpoint was that his head wear was beyond comparison.

2) Have a look at the <u>two texts</u> below. They're both about 'etiquette' — the way that people should <u>behave</u> in certain circumstances.

Source A — 19th-century etiquette guide

The way you behave when out in society is paramount. No matter the situation, it is always essential that you show the highest level of social refinement possible. For example, if someone offers you their hand, take it. Always remove your hat when entering a building. Be punctual to all social events to which you are invited, but take care not to arrive too early.

At most social events, the ability to make good conversation is key. Your discourse must be interesting, but not at all controversial — unless you are talking to a very close friend, avoid incendiary topics such as politics, religion or money. Always greet your host and ask after their well-being, but be careful not to monopolise their time.

Writers' points of view
In Source A, the word 'paramount' suggests that the writer takes etiquette <u>seriously</u>. The writer of Source B, in contrast, says they're 'no stickler for etiquette' which suggests they take it <u>less seriously</u>.

Writers' language
Both writers want the reader to feel like the text is <u>aimed</u> directly at them. Source A uses the <u>pronoun</u> 'you' to do this, whereas Source B uses <u>rhetorical questions</u>.

Writers' language
Source A uses <u>formal language</u> like 'discourse'. In contrast, Source B uses <u>informal language</u> like 'claptrap'. This shows that Source B has a more <u>relaxed</u> tone than Source A.

Source B — 21st-century newspaper article

Anyone who's ever taken a ride on the London Underground will know that there are some rude people out there. I'm no stickler for etiquette, but when I see people refusing to give their seat up to an elderly passenger, it really makes my blood boil. I mean, it's just common courtesy, isn't it? Is it really so difficult to just be a little more civil?

I'm not saying we should all rush back to the stuffy, etiquette-obsessed way that our grandparents did things. All that claptrap sounds dull as dishwater to me. But helping the elderly isn't just polite. It's basic respect for the people who helped build the society that we live in today. I think that's worth spending a few minutes standing up for, don't you?

Writers' points of view
The writers are both <u>considerate</u> of other people's feelings. The writer in Source A thinks it's important to ask about the 'well-being' of a host, and the writer in Source B thinks that helping the elderly is 'basic respect'.

I'd like to compare this pair of pears...

Being able to compare texts is a really important skill. Make sure you practise finding similarities and differences between two texts, and remember to include those all-important linking words.

Answering Writing Questions

These two pages are all about how to write a great answer to question 5 on both papers.

Work out your purpose and audience

See pages 24-25 for more on purpose and audience.

1) For the writing questions, you need to think about the purpose and audience you're writing for.

2) For both papers, question 5 will let you know what they are.
   It won't always be immediately obvious, though:

PAPER 1

This question tells you the audience — it's 'young people aged 14-18'.

| 0 | 5 |

You are going to submit a short story to a magazine. The magazine is aimed at young people aged 14-18.

Write a short story about somebody who has travelled a long way.

The purpose is less obvious here, but because it's a story, you can work out that the purpose is to entertain.

PAPER 2

In this question, you're writing a broadsheet newspaper article, so your audience will mostly be well-educated adults.

| 0 | 5 |

'Students should attend classes virtually. In today's digital society, students shouldn't need to leave the house to go to school.'

Write a broadsheet newspaper article in which you explain your point of view on this statement.

If a question asks you to explain your point of view, then your purpose is to argue.

Jot down your main ideas before you start writing

Only spend about 5 minutes on your plan — don't go into too much detail.

1) Once you've worked out your purpose and audience, you should plan your answers.

2) This will help you to make sure your answers have a clear structure, and that you answer the question that's been asked.

3) Have a look at this example for some ideas:

PAPER 2

| 0 | 5 |

'Modern music glorifies violent lifestyles and should be banned.'

Write a speech, to be delivered in your school assembly, in which you argue for or against this statement.

Purpose and audience
Your points need to be appropriate for the purpose (to argue) and the audience (students).

PLAN

Intro — "My fellow students" etc. don't listen to critics - golden era of music.

Para 2 — Not all modern music glorifies violence - give examples.

Para 3 — It's not just modern music - old music did this too. Give examples.

Para 4 — People aren't robots - won't just become violent by listening to music.

Conc — Critics = out of touch. Not listening to mod. music.

Argument
Make sure you know which side you're arguing for before you start.

Structure
Briefly outline what each paragraph will focus on.

Detail
To save time, write in note form.

Answering Writing Questions

Choose your tone and style to suit your purpose

1) To get good marks, you need to show that you can <u>change</u> the <u>tone</u> and <u>style</u> of your writing to suit your purpose.

See pages 40-41 for more on tone and style.

2) For example, a text written to <u>advise</u> might have a <u>balanced</u>, <u>serious</u> tone:

> *After consulting local residents, and in light of their strong disapproval, this committee recommends that the proposal be withdrawn immediately.* → This text uses <u>formal</u>, <u>complex</u> language to make its advice seem <u>reliable</u>.

3) A <u>persuasive</u> text might be more <u>personal</u>:

> *Like me, <u>you</u> must be weary of criticism. We understand the issues threatening our planet, so why are <u>we</u> being ignored?* → This text uses the pronouns 'you' and 'we' to <u>involve</u> and <u>persuade</u> its audience.

Your tone and style also need to suit your audience

1) You'll also need to <u>adapt</u> your <u>tone</u> and <u>style</u> so that they're <u>appropriate</u> for your <u>audience</u>.

2) Here are a few things you might consider about your <u>audience</u>:

Age	Relationship with reader	Knowledge
• If you're addressing a <u>younger</u> audience, you might use a more <u>light-hearted</u> tone with a <u>conversational</u> style. • A <u>serious</u> tone might be better for <u>older</u> audiences.	• If you're writing to a <u>familiar</u> audience, such as your year group at school, you might use a <u>casual</u>, <u>personal</u> tone. • If you're writing to an <u>unknown</u> audience, you might use an <u>impersonal</u> tone and <u>formal</u> language.	• Different audiences will <u>know</u> different amounts about a subject. • A text aimed at an audience of <u>experts</u> might use more <u>specialised</u> language than a text aimed at a <u>general</u> audience.

3) Whoever your audience is, you should always aim to show off your <u>writing skills</u> to the examiner.

4) Try to avoid <u>common words</u> (such as 'good' and 'nice') that are used lots in everyday language — swap them for something more <u>interesting</u> instead.

See pages 48-49 for more about sentence structures.

5) Always use a <u>range</u> of different <u>sentence structures</u>.

Just try not to sound like you've swallowed a thesaurus...

You need to use a range of words, but too much fancy vocabulary can make your writing hard to understand. Make sure you read back over your work carefully to check this hasn't happened.

Spelling, Punctuation and Grammar

Using correct SPaG (spelling, punctuation and grammar) is really important in your exams.

Make sure you spell words correctly

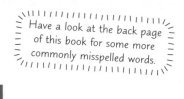
Have a look at the back page of this book for some more commonly misspelled words.

1) Make sure you avoid common spelling mistakes like these:

we're / wear / where

- We're is short for 'we are'.
- Wear is what you do with clothes, shoes and jewellery.
- Where is used for places and positions.

they're / their / there

- They're is short for 'they are'.
- Their is used to talk about something that belongs to somebody. E.g. 'their clothes are wet.'
- There goes with where. It's about places and positions.

accept / except

- Accept is a verb — it means to agree with or receive something. E.g. "The victims accepted compensation."
- Except means not including. E.g. "I like all subjects except for Chemistry."

affect / effect

- Affect is a verb — it describes an action which influences something. E.g. "The broken ankle affected her ability to walk without crutches".
- Effect is a noun. It's the result of something else. E.g. "The text's language has a calming effect on the reader."

2) Using technical terms will get you marks, but it's important to spell them correctly. For example:

- onomatopoeia has four 'o's.
- alliteration has two 'l's.
- metaphor is spelt with a 'ph', not an 'f'.
- rhetorical has an 'h' in it.

Use the right punctuation for the sentence

1) Start every sentence with a capital letter.

2) Make sure you've used full stops at the end of sentences, and question marks at the end of questions.

3) Apostrophes are used when you miss out part of a word, e.g. 'do not' becomes 'don't'. They're also used to show when something belongs to somebody, e.g. 'John's coat'. They are never used for plurals.

4) Remember 'it's' (with an apostrophe) is short for 'it is'. 'Its' (without an apostrophe) means 'belonging to

It's bad to lie to your friends.	*"It's real!" she insisted.*	*Put the cake in its box.*	*The fish has lost its scales.*

5) You should use commas when:

- you want to separate items in a list. ⟹ *We bought eggs, butter, flour and sugar.*
- you've used more than one adjective. ⟹ *The stale, dry sausage roll tasted awful.*
- you need to separate some extra information. ⟹ *Ranjita, who is older than Asha, was less upset.*

6) Use speech marks (" ") to show where you've quoted from a text, or when someone is speaking out loud

Section Two — Do Well in your Exams

Spelling, Punctuation and Grammar

Avoid these common grammar mistakes

1) Don't change <u>tenses</u> in the middle of your writing.

| *The writer suggests that you shouldn't buy organic vegetables — he said that they're "too expensive".* → | These tenses don't <u>match</u>. 'Suggests' is in the <u>present tense</u>, but 'said' is in the <u>past tense</u> — it should be 'says'. |

2) Don't use <u>double negatives</u>, e.g. 'There <u>wasn't no</u> reason' should be 'There <u>wasn't any</u> reason'.

3) Never write 'should of', 'could of' or 'would of' — it's always '<u>should have</u>', '<u>could have</u>' or '<u>would have</u>'.

4) Don't mix up '<u>them</u>' and '<u>those</u>'. '<u>Them</u>' should <u>never</u> be used before a noun:

| *I hate <u>them</u> cats.* → | This is <u>wrong</u> — <u>cats</u> is a noun, and you shouldn't use '<u>them</u>' with a noun. |
| *I hate <u>those</u> cats.* → | In sentences like this, use '<u>those</u>' instead. |

Aggie was particularly good at remembering which witch was which.

Check over your work when you've finished

1) Try to leave a few minutes at the <u>end</u> of each exam to <u>check</u> your work.

2) Start by checking your answers to the <u>writing questions</u> (question 5 on both papers).

3) There might not be <u>time</u> to check everything in detail. Look for the <u>most obvious</u> spelling, punctuation and grammar mistakes.

4) Here are some <u>mistakes</u> you could look for:

- Check that your words have been written out <u>in full</u>. Use '<u>for example</u>' instead of 'e.g.', and always write the word '<u>and</u>' out fully — don't use '&' or '+'.

- Check for anything that's not written in <u>Standard English</u> — you shouldn't have used any <u>text speak</u> (like 'cos' instead of 'because').

- Check you haven't <u>repeated</u> a word too many times in one sentence. For example, you might change "beef <u>and</u> chicken <u>and</u> fish" to "beef, chicken and fish".

5) If you find a mistake, correct it <u>neatly</u> — make sure the examiner can <u>read</u> what you've written.

I wish I hadn't had beef for dinner — it was a miss-steak...

Think about your exam timings. If you don't plan your time properly, you'll end up rushing to finish, which will mean you're more likely to make silly SPaG errors. Plus, it's just plain stressful...

Section Two — Do Well in your Exams

Purpose and Audience

You need to know how to pick out the purpose of a text — that's the writer's reason for writing a text. You also need to be able to work out a text's audience — the people who are supposed to read it.

There are four common purposes

The information on these two pages will help you with questions 2, 3 and 4 on paper 1, and questions 3 and 4 on paper 2.

1) The <u>purpose</u> of a text is the <u>reason</u> that it's been written.

2) Most texts are written for one of these <u>purposes</u>:

To Inform

They <u>tell</u> the reader about something:

The weather today will be sunny.

To Advise

They <u>help</u> the reader to <u>do something</u>:

To fix a broken vase, first gather together all the broken pieces.

To Argue or Persuade

They try to make the reader <u>agree</u> with the writer's <u>opinion</u>:

We must ban animal testing immediately.

To Entertain

They are <u>enjoyable</u>, <u>interesting</u> or <u>exciting</u> for the reader:

Harry edged into the cave, trying his best to ignore the shiver that ran down his spine as he left the daylight behind.

3) The purpose of most <u>non-fiction</u> texts is usually quite <u>obvious</u>. For example, a speech might openly try to <u>persuade</u> the listener to do something.

4) The purpose of most <u>fiction</u> texts is to <u>entertain</u> the reader.

5) Some texts can have <u>more than one</u> purpose. For example, a <u>letter</u> could aim to <u>inform</u> and <u>entertain</u>.

Barry's porpoise in life had always been to entertain.

Writers always have an audience in mind

1) The <u>audience</u> is the <u>group of people</u> that the writer is <u>aiming</u> their writing at.

2) The audience can be <u>general</u>. For example, a text might be aimed at <u>adults</u>.

3) The audience can also be more <u>specific</u>. For example, a text might <u>only</u> be aimed at <u>car drivers</u>.

4) Some texts can have <u>more than one</u> audience. For example, a children's book might be aimed at the <u>children</u> who will read it <u>and</u> the <u>adults</u> who will buy it for them.

5) You can <u>work out</u> the audience of a text by looking at:

- the <u>content</u> (what it's <u>about</u>)
- the <u>vocabulary</u> (the <u>words</u> it uses).

Dungeon Killer 3 is the hottest game of the year! There are 52 awesome levels and 6 cool new characters — don't miss out on this wild new gaming experience!

- This text is <u>about</u> a video game, so its audience is people who are <u>interested in video games</u>.
- It uses <u>informal words</u> like "<u>awesome</u>" and "<u>cool</u>", so it's probably aimed at a <u>young</u> audience.

Purpose and Audience

Always keep the purpose and audience in mind

1) In your exam answers, it's important to write about how texts are adapted to their purpose and audience.

Here are some things to think about:

- How the writer's choice of language would be interesting for the audience.
- How the writer's choice of language helps them to achieve their purpose.
- How the text's structure might be interesting for the audience.
- How the text's structure helps the writer to achieve their purpose.

2) Have a look at this text — it's like one you could get in your exams:

Audience — British people
This text is aimed at people who live in Britain.

Audience — busy adults
This sentence is about travelling to work, looking after children and getting ready for the day. This shows that the text is aimed at adults who are so busy that they don't have time for breakfast.

Audience — parents
The text has a separate paragraph about making sure that children eat breakfast. This structure suggests that it's aimed at parents.

WHY BOTHER WITH BREAKFAST?

David Barowsky, nutritional analyst

Eating breakfast improves mental and physical performance.

This is a well-known and incontrovertible fact. And yet, a recent study has revealed that 20 million of us Brits regularly skip this essential refuelling opportunity. Why is this the case?

Are we too busy commuting, getting the kids ready for school, blow-drying our hair? Do you often feel frantic and harassed in the morning? Well, the time has come to change your ways. Breakfast does not have to be an elaborate or time-consuming meal. Allow ten minutes extra for a nutritious bowl of porridge or granola every morning, and the benefits will be noticeable almost immediately.

Another troubling trend is the rising number of children and teenagers who don't eat breakfast before leaving for school or college. Allowing your kids to skip breakfast is reckless and irresponsible. You are simply not providing them with the energy they need to face the day. Set a good example by eating breakfast yourself, and make sure you build a morning meal into your children's daily routine as soon as possible.

Purpose — to persuade
This text is using 'us', which persuades the reader by making them feel involved.

Purpose — to persuade
Rhetorical questions like these persuade the reader by making them think about their own experiences or opinions.

Purpose — to persuade
This language persuades the reader by making them feel bad.

Purpose — to advise
This is giving an instruction, which suggests that the purpose is partly to advise.

This page was no accident — I wrote it on purpose...

Knowing the audience and purpose will be useful for a lot of the exam questions. You might find it helpful to write down the purpose and audience of each source somewhere on your exam papers.

Purpose and Audience — Questions

Q1   For each sentence, circle the word which best describes its intended audience.

a) "Do you yearn for a simpler, more reliable way of managing your finances?"

children / adults

b) "When buying a used car, try to get as much information from the dealer as you can."

experts / novices

When buying a used toilet roll — don't.

Q2   Draw lines to match each text to its main purpose.

a) "Shop around for the best quote — some insurers are much more expensive than others."

To entertain

b) "As the train moved south, first crawling, then increasing to a steady gallop, the scenery gradually changed from the flat and drab to the dramatic and beautiful."

To persuade

c) "Who could disagree with the fact that children should eat healthily?"

To advise

Q3   Find **two** words or phrases that show this text is aimed at a younger audience, and explain how they show this.

> Are you looking for a cool summer job?
>
> We've got loads of temporary vacancies with no experience required!
>
> All you need is some free time over the holidays, a positive attitude and plenty of energy. If you've got your own wheels that's even better!
>
> With Spondon Summer Jobs you can:
> • gain real-world work experience
> • earn a few quid
> • make new friends
>
> Whatever you fancy, we can find you a job that suits you down to the ground! Interested? Call Jackie on 0547 262 626 or find us on social media.

Word or phrase:..

Explanation: ....

....

Word or phrase:..

Explanation: ....

....

Section Three — Reading: Understanding Texts

Purpose and Audience — Questions

Try these exam-style questions, then use the self-assessment boxes to mark how well you think you did.

Q4 Read the following extract from a leaflet advertising an aquarium.

> **Come to Oxton Aquarium — you'll have a whale of a time!**
>
> At Oxton Aquarium you can see lots of different sea creatures all in one place. You could be eyed up by an octopus, shaken by a shark or peered at by a pike! They're all here in our very special underwater world — and we're open every day in the school holidays!
>
> Whether you come with your school, your family or your friends, you're bound to have a fantastic time.
>
> "I've had the best day ever!" — Adam Rodgers, age 9.
>
> Oxton Aquarium is a fun, fishy day out that you'll never forget!

Helpful tips:

1. Work out <u>who</u> you think the target <u>audience</u> is.

2. <u>Underline</u> any language features that you think would <u>appeal</u> to the audience — have a look at <u>section 5</u> to help you with this.

3. Pick <u>two or three</u> to write about in your answer.

4. Remember to <u>explain how</u> the language features make the text appealing.

How has the writer used language to appeal to their audience?

Q5 Read the following extract from a newspaper opinion piece.

> Is it that time of year again? The decorations have gone up and the nation has whipped itself into a frenzy, wholly convinced that the only way to survive the Christmas season is to go out and panic buy everything in the supermarket, right down to the last parsnip.
> Admit it — the whole thing is ridiculous. Don't get me wrong, I love Christmas. I love the presents, the fun and, most of all, the food.
> But what must change is the way that we frantically race to the shops five minutes before closing on Christmas Eve. We've all been there, right? Running around like headless chickens, gripped by a sudden and deathly terror that we've forgotten the after-dinner mints.
> Britain, we need to take a stand against festive stress. Christmas is a special time of year; it should be a time to sit back and take a break from the trials and tribulations of everyday life. So please, enjoy your holiday — and try to remember that the world won't end should you happen to forget the cranberry sauce.

Don't forget to look at section 5 for help with language features.

How does the writer use language to influence their audience?

Questions that ask about 'influence' want you to write about how the text <u>affects</u> the reader.

 Read the questions first...

Read the exam questions before you start reading the source text. That way, when you read the source, you'll be able to pick out all the features that will help you to answer the questions.

Section Three — Reading: Understanding Texts

Writer's Viewpoint and Attitude

In your exams, you need to work out what the writer is thinking.

Viewpoint and attitude are what the writer thinks

1) The writer's <u>purpose</u> is what they're trying to <u>do</u> with a text — <u>inform</u>, <u>persuade</u>, <u>advise</u> or <u>entertain</u>.

2) The <u>writer's viewpoint</u> (or <u>attitude</u>) is different — it's what the writer <u>thinks</u> about the topic of the text.

> *It isn't fair that some schools make you wear school uniforms and others don't. We should all have to wear school uniforms.*

> The <u>writer's viewpoint</u> is their belief that all students should have to wear a <u>school uniform</u>.

> *Don't listen to all the fuss about chocolate — there is no ice cream flavour that beats vanilla.*

> The <u>writer's viewpoint</u> is that <u>vanilla</u> is the <u>best flavour</u> of ice cream.

3) Writers can sometimes express more <u>complicated</u> viewpoints:

> *As a general rule, I hate all things ocean-related. I can't stand swimming or diving — or seafood, for that matter. But that's never affected the thrill I feel every time I climb aboard a sailboat.*

> The writer dislikes most things about the sea, apart from <u>sailing</u>, which they like a lot.

> Always read questions about viewpoint and attitude carefully so that you know which topic you need to write about.

The writers' viewpoint isn't always obvious

1) Sometimes the writer's viewpoint will be <u>really clear</u> from the text:

> *I think we should stop using semi-colons entirely, and I'm here today to tell you why.*

> This writer <u>states their viewpoint</u> directly. They think we <u>shouldn't</u> use <u>semi-colons</u>.

2) When the writer's viewpoint is <u>less</u> obvious, you can look for clues in the text's <u>language</u>:

> *I visited a beautiful island, which had gorgeous sandy beaches and incredibly clear blue waters.*

> The writer of this text doesn't <u>say</u> that they <u>liked</u> the island, but the words 'beautiful' and 'gorgeous' suggest that they <u>did</u>.

> *The librarian's sinister smile revealed teeth that were like a row of broken tombstones.*

> The word 'sinister' and the <u>simile</u> 'like a row of broken tombstones' <u>hint</u> that the writer finds the librarian <u>scary</u>.

Margaret was starting to get sick of Benji's attitude.

Section Three — Reading: Understanding Texts

Writer's Viewpoint and Attitude

Work out the writer's viewpoint using clues from the text

1) You'll have to compare the viewpoints of two writers for paper 2, question 4.

2) Read these tips to help you answer questions about writers' viewpoints:

- Look at the question to find out which topic you need to write about.

- You need to write about how the writers show their attitudes to the reader, so look for language that shows you what they're thinking or feeling.

- Make sure you include quotes and examples from both texts to support each point you make.

3) Have a look at this exam-style text:

Viewpoint — human knowledge
This word shows that the writer thinks humans becoming 'walking, talking encyclopaedias' is a bad thing.

Viewpoint — imagination
This metaphor helps the reader to understand the writer's viewpoint that the Internet is badly affecting how much people use their imagination.

Viewpoint — the Internet
This comparison shows that the writer doesn't like the Internet.

In today's world we are plagued by information. Gone are the days of blissful ignorance; instead we live in an era of incessant awareness.

The invention of the Internet has brought the full total of the world's knowledge directly to our fingertips. In doing so, it has reduced us to a collection of walking, talking encyclopaedias. We are obsessed with information, and yet the immediate availability of this knowledge has completely extinguished the dying embers of our imagination. No longer do we wonder about anything, spending pleasant hours pondering 'why...' and 'what if...'. We simply look it up, and the information is instantly ours.

I am willing to concede that the Internet might be one of man's most ingenious inventions, but hey, so was the atomic bomb. And, like the atomic bomb, we should treat the Internet as the powerful, dangerous entity that it really is.

Viewpoint — information
This negative language suggests that the writer doesn't like having access to so much information.

Viewpoint — the Internet
On its own, this sentence makes it seem like the writer thinks the Internet is a good thing, but read the whole text before you decide what the writer's viewpoint is. The writer actually finds it frustrating and dangerous.

Viewpoint — the Internet
This statement clearly explains the writer's viewpoint, so the reader knows that the writer fears the Internet.

They told me to find a view point, so I climbed a mountain...

You'll find lots of clues about the writer's viewpoint in the language of a text. Make sure you read your sources carefully so that you can spot these clues and write about them in your answers.

Section Three — Reading: Understanding Texts

Writer's Viewpoint and Attitude — Questions

Q1   Read these play reviews. Write down whether each attitude is **positive**, **negative** or **balanced**.

   a) This playwright's recent offerings on the London stage had established
   high expectations, but his latest "masterpiece" falls far short of that hype.   ....

   b) I have never left a matinee performance and rushed straight
   to the box office to buy a ticket for that evening. Until now.   ....

   c) I can't say I was dazzled, but I certainly wasn't disappointed.
   A pleasant evening, if not one to write home about.   ....

Q2   Draw lines to match the extracts below to the viewpoints they're expressing.

   a) *"I've always considered mixed schools to
   be a barrier to educational progress. We
   should all stick with traditional segregation."*

   b) *"Mixed schools are clearly superior,
   but parents should have a choice."*

   c) *"It's time we ended outdated single-sex
   education. Mixed schools are the future."*

   i) Prefers mixed schools and thinks
   single-sex schools should be abolished.

   ii) Prefers mixed schools but thinks single-sex
   schools should still be an option.

   iii) Dislikes mixed schools and thinks
   all schools should be single-sex.

Q3   Summarise **one** thing that these two writers agree on, and **one** thing that
   they disagree on. Use evidence from the text to support your answer.

   Source A Mobile phone disruptions in
   lessons are a nightmare for any teacher.
   Surely the best way to prevent this is
   simply to ban them from school entirely.

   Source B I'm not about to suggest that students
   should be permitted to use mobiles during
   lessons, but I fail to see that any harm can be
   caused by allowing them during lunchtimes.

   The writers agree that ....

   ....

   ....

   The writers disagree that ....

   ....

   ....

Section Three — Reading: Understanding Texts

Writer's Viewpoint and Attitude — Questions

Answer these exam practice questions, then tick the boxes underneath to say how confident you feel.

Q4   Read the following extract, which is from a newspaper article written in the 20th century.

> The London art scene has rarely been so <mark>exciting.</mark> We are seeing a real increase in the number of artists who aren't afraid to throw off <mark>the iron shackles of 'traditional art'</mark> and <mark>celebrate self-expression.</mark> They're rule breakers, unafraid of the giants of the past. They're <mark>revolutionaries,</mark> constantly looking forward, never back. Only by pushing the boundaries of modern art are we going to see any positive growth in the field. <mark>When art conforms, it becomes lifeless,</mark> and these new experimenters understand that.

To get you started, some key words and phrases have been highlighted.

How has the writer conveyed their attitude towards art?

Q5   Read the following extracts. Source A is an extract from a diary written in the 19th century, and Source B is from a speech written in the 21st century.

Source A

Dear Diary —

   We took a trip to see the new steam train today, which was being exhibited in James Square. It was fascinating — a clanking steel giant, shiny as a new penny, with a great puff of steam that emerged from its funnel and curled into the summer sky. To think, Daddy says one day they may be able to carry people from one end of the country to the other! I for one cannot wait.

Source B

Residents of Station Crescent! I know that you, like me, are plagued day-in, day-out with the sounds, smells and sights of the railway. Like me, many of you moved here at a time when three or four trains a day passed by, barely disturbing us at all. And like me, you've seen our area systematically invaded by a non-stop army of trains, impacting our quality of life — not to mention the price of our homes.

Compare how the writers convey their different attitudes towards rail transport.

In your answer, you should:

- compare their different attitudes
- compare the methods they use to convey their attitudes
- support your ideas with quotations from both texts.

Make sure your answer includes everything that's mentioned in these bullet points.

EXAM TIP

Write about __how__ the writer is expressing their viewpoint...

Remember, you need to go beyond just __what__ the writer's viewpoint is — you need to think about __how__ they're expressing it, too. Comment on how they use language to show their viewpoint.

Section Three — Reading: Understanding Texts

Finding Information and Ideas

Finding information in texts can be quite straightforward. There are a few key things to keep in mind, though

Some questions ask you to pick out information

1) <u>Question 1</u> in each paper is all about <u>finding information</u>.

2) The information you pick out will either be <u>explicit</u> or <u>implicit</u>.

3) <u>Explicit</u> information is <u>clearly written</u> in the text:

"It rained HOW much?"

> *Last weekend, it rained a lot.* ⟶ The text <u>says</u> that it rained, so we know that it rained.

> *The tall man made me a sandwich.* ⟶ This text <u>tells you</u> that the man is <u>tall</u>, and he made the writer a <u>sandwich</u>.

4) <u>Implicit</u> information <u>isn't immediately obvious</u> — you have to <u>work it out</u> from what the text says:

> *The castle was dark, damp and freezing cold.* ⟶ This <u>implies</u> that the writer doesn't like the castle, even though it isn't made <u>explicit</u> in the text.

> *When she saw her present, Emelia let out a loud shriek and hugged May tightly.* ⟶ Emelia's reaction to the present <u>implies</u> that she is excited about it.

> *Jake had come straight from the cinema, where his manager had been telling him off for not cleaning the popcorn machine properly.* ⟶ In this text, it's <u>implied</u> that Jake works at the cinema, but the text doesn't state this <u>directly</u>.

Use underlining to help you answer fact-finding questions

1) Always read the <u>questions</u> before you read the sources, so you know what to look for <u>as you read</u>.

2) If you only need to look for information from a <u>part</u> of the text, draw a <u>box</u> around it so that you don't look for facts in the <u>wrong</u> bit.

3) As you read, <u>underline</u> information in the text that's <u>relevant</u> to the <u>question</u>.

> If you had to find <u>facts</u> about the <u>town</u> in this text, you could pick out these points: ⟶ *At the age of 46, I sold my house and rented a cottage in the <u>idyllic Scottish town</u> where I grew up. After just a few weeks, I knew I'd made the right decision: <u>Melrose</u>, with its <u>friendly people</u> and <u>stunning scenery</u>, is a <u>wonderful place to live</u>.*

4) Look back at your <u>underlined text</u> to help you answer the question.

Finding Information and Ideas

Pick information from the right part of the text

1) Here are some <u>tips</u> to help you answer fact-finding questions:

> - <u>Read</u> the question carefully, so that you only pick out information about the <u>right topic</u>.
> - Make sure you either shade the <u>right number of boxes</u>, or write down the <u>right number of facts</u>.
> - If the question mentions <u>line numbers</u>, make sure you only use information from <u>those lines</u>.
> - Double-check your answers against the <u>sources</u> so that you don't make any <u>mistakes</u>.

2) Now have a look at this <u>exam-style text</u>.

Implicit information about Brian
This text is in the <u>past tense</u>. This tells the reader that Brian doesn't go to school <u>any more</u>.

Implicit information about the school
This suggests that the <u>heating system</u> in the school didn't work very well.

Brian had hated school. He often thought back to the dreary breezeblock walls, the freezing classrooms and the constant drone of the centuries-old plumbing.

St Mary's had been the closest school to Brian's house, but that was an all-girls school. This meant that every morning Brian had had to withstand the torment of a fifteen-minute bus journey across town to Beeches Hall — the boys' school. This bus journey would have been perfectly tolerable had it not been for the driver: a peculiar, unpleasant man with a severely erratic driving style.

Explicit information about the journey
This tells the reader that Brian's bus took <u>fifteen minutes</u> to get to Beeches Hall.

Explicit information about the bus
This says that the <u>steps</u> on to the bus were made of <u>steel</u>.

Every morning, after he'd climbed the steel steps of the bus, Brian would be greeted by the driver's stormy frown, as if Brian's presence on his sacred vehicle was the greatest possible offence. Trying desperately to avoid eye contact, Brian would thrust his 50p in the driver's direction and hurriedly remove himself from his angry glare before it was too late.

Implicit information about Brian
These phrases <u>imply</u> that Brian was <u>afraid</u> of the bus driver.

He always considered himself lucky if he managed to find a seat before the bus screeched off again, charging through the streets like a raging bull.

Implicit information about the bus
This <u>simile</u> suggests that the bus was moving <u>quickly</u> and <u>powerfully</u>.

Not quite as exciting as finding buried treasure...

You'll definitely have to find some information and ideas for question 1 on both papers. Being able to spot implicit information will also help you to write answers for the other reading questions.

Finding Information and Ideas — Questions

Q1 Read the text below.

> Dani approached the roller coaster with wide eyes. She had never been a big fan of rides, but her friend Mel had offered to give £20 to charity if Dani agreed to ride the biggest roller coaster in the park — a towering steel beast with four loops and six corkscrew turns. Her stomach churned at the thought.
> "You can do it, Dani," Mel said, squeezing her shoulder. "You might even enjoy it!"

Dani kept insisting she wasn't a big fan, but the evidence was all there...

Tick the **one** statement that is true.

a) Dani's friend Mel loves theme park rides. ☐

b) Dani is nervous about going on the roller coaster. ☐

c) It was Dani's idea to get sponsored to go on the ride. ☐

Q2 Underline the words and phrases which show that the writer has a negative view of the zoo.

> Last weekend we found ourselves with nothing to do on a warm, sunny day, so we decided on a trip to the zoo. The entrance to the zoo was via a rusty iron gate that looked in serious need of repair. We went into the ticket office, only to discover that the floor was filthy; as we looked closer, we realised there was revolting leftover food scattered everywhere. Inside, the animals looked malnourished and miserable in their enclosures, which all seemed dull and empty, with precious little space for them to run around. All in all, a pretty depressing place.

Q3 From lines 3-8 of the text below, write down **three** facts about the garden.

> 1   "If the boiler hadn't broken, we'd have enough money to go to Hawaii by now," said
> 2 Tim glumly, skirting a puddle of mud in order to peg the laundry onto the washing line.
> 3   Alex frowned and sat down heavily on the bench, which took up almost all of the
> 4 space in their tiny back garden.
> 5   "I bet it's sunny there," she said wistfully, pulling her cardigan in closer.
> 6   The wind was whistling a discordant chorus through the gaps in the fence, making
> 7 the damp grass shiver. The gnarled, stunted apple tree in the corner emitted an
> 8 ominously loud groan that made Tim jump.

1)..

2)..

3)..

Finding Information and Ideas — Questions

Now you've got the theory sorted, it's time to put it into practice with these exam-style questions.

Q4   Read the following extract from a review of a holiday park, then tick **three** statements that are **true**.

> You would need a fortnight to try all the activities at Lowbridge Park. There's so much to try, from abseiling to zorbing. I was only there for a weekend, so I had to prioritise!
>
> I began with a pony trek. Although it drizzled the entire morning, it was a great way to explore. In the afternoon I debated between rock climbing and mountain biking. I settled on the former, primarily to stay out of the rain!
>
> The next day, the weather was much better, so my choice fell between canoeing and sailing. I went for a canoe and headed to the lake, which was stunning early in the morning.
>
> I finished my weekend with some archery. I'm no Robin Hood, but the instructor was very patient with me, and I'm pleased to say I improved a little as time went by.

1. The writer went mountain biking. ☐

2. On the second day, the writer got up early. ☐

3. The writer had time to try everything. ☐

4. The writer enjoyed the pony trek. ☐

5. The weather stayed sunny all weekend. ☐

6. You can abseil at Lowbridge Park. ☐

Q5   Read the following extract from a novel.

> The doorbell rang. Someone must have answered it, because moments later I heard George's nasal tones in the hallway.
>
> "So lovely to be here!" he cried, his voice carrying easily across the living room.
>
> "Did you invite him?" I hissed, staring desperately at Rosa.
>
> "I could hardly leave him out," she said coolly. "It would have been too obvious."
>
> He entered the room. His garish purple suit and elaborate hairstyle made him stand out sharply from the other guests. "You made it!" Rosa cooed to him.
>
> "Rosa!" he said, presenting her with a bottle of wine. "And Freddie," he said to me, extending a greasy hand adorned with several gaudy rings. "Good to see you."
>
> "You too," I said, forcing a smile and letting go of his hand quickly. "Drink?"
>
> "Oh, go on then," said George, "I'd love a nice whisky, if you have any?"
>
> "Nothing but the best for you, George," I replied through gritted teeth.

This question is asking you about George. All your facts need to be about him.

List **four** facts from the text about George.

Practise looking for information and ideas...

The most useful way to revise for question 1 is to practise, practise, practise. Read some texts at home (such as newspaper articles or short stories) and pick out facts and ideas from each one.

Summarising Information and Ideas

You need to be able to summarise information for paper 2, question 2. Read on to find out more...

Summaries are about choosing and explaining information

1) A summary is a <u>short account</u> of a lot of information.

2) To write a <u>summary</u>, you need to <u>choose information</u> from a text about a <u>particular topic</u>, then write about it in your <u>own words</u>.

The information might be <u>implicit</u> or <u>explicit</u> (there's more about this on p.32).

3) For paper 2, question 2, you'll be asked to summarise the <u>similarities</u> or <u>differences</u> between <u>two</u> texts. This is the same as <u>comparing</u> two texts (see pages 18-19).

4) You'll be asked to write a summary about <u>two characters</u>, or a <u>topic</u> that the texts have in common.

5) For example, if you were asked to summarise the <u>differences</u> between the <u>characters</u> in these texts...

> **Source A**
> Gemma put on her <u>freshly ironed</u> dress, brushed her hair, then carefully replaced the hairbrush in the chest of drawers.

> **Source B**
> Holly ignored her hairbrush completely. Instead, she grabbed a <u>tatty</u>, <u>old</u> hat and jammed it over her unruly hair.

... you could write a <u>point</u> like this:

> *Gemma takes better care of her appearance than Holly. For example, Gemma's clothes are "<u>freshly ironed</u>", which suggests they're neat and clean. In contrast, Holly's hat is described as "<u>tatty</u>" and "<u>old</u>", which suggests it's not very neat or clean. This has the effect of making Holly seem like she doesn't care about the way she dresses, unlike Gemma, who clearly does care.*

Think about the structure of your answer

1) Always write in <u>paragraphs</u> to <u>structure</u> your summaries.

2) When writing a summary of two texts, you could write a <u>whole paragraph</u> about one text, then a paragraph about the <u>other</u>.

3) Or you could write about <u>both texts</u> in the <u>same paragraph</u>.

4) However you structure your answer, make sure that you:

- make points that are <u>relevant</u> to <u>both</u> texts

- include <u>examples</u> from both texts

- explain <u>how</u> each example you use shows a similarity or difference between the texts.

5) You can use <u>linking words</u> to make your comparisons clear, for example:

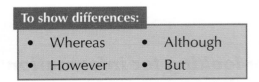

To show similarities:
- Similarly
- Equally
- Likewise
- Also

To show differences:
- Whereas
- However
- Although
- But

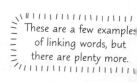

These are a few examples of linking words, but there are plenty more.

Summarising Information and Ideas

Back up your points with examples from the texts

1) Have a look at this advice to help you with exam questions on summarising information:

> • Write in full sentences and use your own words to summarise the similarities or differences between the two texts.
>
> • Structure your answer using paragraphs and linking words to make your comparisons really clear.
>
> • Make sure you back up your points with plenty of examples from both texts.

2) Have a look at the two texts below. They're each about a boy who has been told off by his father.

3) The notes highlight some of the similarities and differences between the boys.

Source A — 20th-century diary

Friday 21 March 1947

What an eventful afternoon. Daddy shouted at me just for being late to school. "You're thirteen now, Andrew, you should be more responsible!" he was yelling. I had to try not to laugh at first — he looks so funny when he's shouting, because he goes red in the face.

It stopped being as funny when he said he had half a mind to stop wasting his money on my private education. I'd never admit it to Daddy, but that did upset me a little bit.

Difference
Richard and Andrew are from different time periods and are different ages, so they might have different attitudes or viewpoints.

Difference
Richard has a more respectful relationship with his father than Andrew. Richard 'sat quietly' as his father told him off, whereas Andrew's first instinct was to 'laugh' at his angry father.

Difference
Richard's family have 'little money', but Andrew's family can afford a 'private education'.

Similarity
Andrew tries to hide his emotions from his father. Richard's short response could imply that he's also trying not to show his feelings.

Source B — 19th-century diary

Saturday 12 September 1868

Today we held Richard's 16th birthday party. We had made decorations and Mother had baked a cake, but in the end it was not such a celebration.

Richard sat quietly all evening, his hands folded in his lap, as Father lectured us for hours on end about how he believed the party was a waste of the little money we have. Richard said almost nothing in response. He only broke his silence to acknowledge Father's tirade with a quiet "Yes, Sir".

Think of it as a less fun version of spot the difference...

As part of your revision, you could try practising your own summarising skills using the texts above. Have a go at writing down some similarities and differences between the two fathers, for example.

Summarising — Questions

Q1   Read the text below.

> "We're going to be late, Samuel," warned Rita, biting her thumbnail nervously.
> "We'll be fine!" insisted Samuel from the depths of his wardrobe. After a moment he emerged, triumphantly holding his favourite leather jacket aloft.
> Rita glared pointedly at her watch, then at Samuel, who grinned.
> "We'll be fine," he repeated, trying on the jacket and admiring his reflection in the full-length mirror.
> "It's bad enough that we have to go at all, and now we're going to show up late too," complained Rita. "This is all your fault. If it were up to me, we'd never have agreed to go. I hated that school."
> "Oh, cheer up, Rita — it's a reunion, not a funeral," said Samuel. "It'll be fun!"

Circle whether each of the following statements refers to Samuel or Rita, then write down a quote on the dotted line to support your choice.

a) The character who is reluctant to go to the reunion.   (Samuel / Rita)

....

b) The character who cares most about time management.   (Samuel / Rita)

....

c) The more confident character in the extract.   (Samuel / Rita)

....

Q2   Summarise the two views given in the text below.

> Human beings have eaten meat for millions of years. Meat eaters argue that we have evolved with the ability to eat and digest meat, proving that it forms a natural part of the human diet. Furthermore, meat contains many vitamins and minerals, particularly iron, that are important for human function.
> However, vegetarians argue that, biologically, we have very little in common with other species of meat eaters. For example, we lack the ability to kill an animal and take its meat without tools. Additionally, they argue that a high consumption of red meat contributes to a range of health problems in humans, such as cardiovascular disease and some cancers.

Meat Eaters: ....

....

Vegetarians: ....

....

Summarising — Questions

Here are some exam practice questions. Don't forget to tick an assessment box when you're done.

Q3 Read the following extract from a diary written in the 20th century.

> Today I've been helping at an underfunded local orphanage, which was built for kids who lost their families in the influenza epidemic. It's been incredibly **sad** to see so many children having to live in such basic conditions. **It's not that surprising** though, given the living conditions in general in this area — lots of houses don't have any running water at all, and it's fairly common to see large families all living together in one room.
>
> They need donations desperately, so **I'll give what I can.** But really, it's **their government who should be providing for them.**

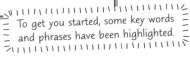
To get you started, some key words and phrases have been highlighted.

Summarise the writer's viewpoint on the orphanage.

Q4 Read the following extracts. Source A is from a housekeeping magazine written in the 19th century, and Source B is from a newspaper article that was written in the 21st century.

Source A

The secret to a harmonious marriage lies in the willingness of the wife to be amenable to the needs of the husband.

A good wife will not pester her husband, nor will she bore him with gossip or domestic trivialities. Instead, she will endeavour to be sweet and charming, always fulfilling his needs. If he wishes to complain, she should listen; if he seeks quiet, she should be silent. The home is her sphere, and she should strive to make it a haven for him, in which he need not lift a finger.

Source B

In the 21st century, a marriage is a partnership of equals. Today, it is common for both members of a couple to work full-time. This means that it is essential for domestic responsibilities to be shared evenly too. Whilst housework was once considered the domain of women, most women today would spurn the idea that they should work full-time and take sole care of a home. Men are just as capable of cleaning and cooking as women, and fortunately many modern husbands have realised this crucial fact.

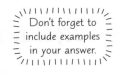
Don't forget to include examples in your answer.

Summarise the differences between the views given in Source A and Source B.

Write notes to help you...

For questions about summarising, it might help you to underline bits of the texts. You could also try making a quick table at the top of your answer booklet, to help you compare the two sources.

Section Four — Reading: Information and Ideas

Tone and Style

This information on tone and style will be useful for all of the reading questions on both papers.

Tone is to do with feeling

1) A text's tone is the <u>feeling</u> it's written with. For example, the tone could be:

> • happy • sad • serious • funny • excited • calm

Think of a writer's tone as being like someone's tone of voice when they're talking.

2) The <u>language</u> of a text shows what the tone is. For example:

| *It'd be great if you could help us out with this.* → | <u>Informal</u> language like 'It'd' and 'help us out' give this example a <u>friendly</u> tone. |

3) The <u>purpose</u> of the text might affect the writer's choice of tone:

| *The event will take place on Wednesday afternoon.* → | This sentence has an <u>unemotional</u> tone. This suits its purpose of <u>informing</u> the reader in a <u>straightforward</u> way. |

4) A writer might also choose their tone based on their <u>audience</u>:

| *So book a flight, grab your board and get out to the Alps before all that snow melts! You just know you wanna!* → | The use of <u>exclamation marks</u> and <u>informal</u> language such as 'grab' give this an <u>excited</u> tone. This might suit a <u>young</u> audience. |

"You will not take that tone with me, good Sir Knight!"

Style is how the text is written

1) A text's <u>style</u> is the way it's written. This includes:

- <u>language choices</u> — the <u>words</u>, <u>phrases</u> and <u>language techniques</u> that are used
- <u>sentence forms</u> — the <u>length</u> or <u>type</u> of sentences used
- <u>structure</u> — the way texts are <u>organised</u>.

See section 6 for more about the structure of texts.

2) There are lots of <u>different styles</u> a text can have. Here are a couple of examples:

| *It'll be rubbish when the leisure centre shuts.* → | Using words that are often used in <u>informal spoken</u> language (such as 'rubbish') creates a <u>conversational style</u>. |

| *Supporters of the new housing development say it will help to meet the ever-increasing demand for homes in the town. Many residents, however, oppose the development, claiming it will reduce the amount of recreational green space available.* → | This provides two <u>opposing views</u> of the housing development, giving the news report a <u>balanced structure</u>. This is known as <u>journalistic style</u>. |

3) Writers <u>choose</u> their style to suit the <u>purpose</u> and <u>audience</u> of a text.

Tone and Style

Say why the writer has used that tone and style

1) In the <u>exam</u>, it's not enough to just spot what the <u>tone</u> or <u>style</u> is.

2) You need to explain <u>why</u> a writer has used a certain tone or style.
   Try to think about:

   - What <u>effect</u> the tone and style might have on the <u>audience</u>.
   - How the tone and style help the writer to <u>achieve</u> their <u>purpose</u>.
   - What the tone and style might <u>suggest</u> about the writer's <u>attitude</u>.

3) Have a look at the <u>text</u> below:

Friendly tone
This informal phrase and the use of positive language such as 'great' creates a <u>friendly</u> tone.

Conversational style
Informal language such as 'Brits' gives the letter a laid-back, <u>conversational</u> style.

Personal tone
This phrase speaks to the reader in a direct and personal way, which shows that the writer <u>knows the reader well</u>.

Relaxed tone
Informal language like 'a little bit' gives the letter a relaxed tone. This means that, although the writer is giving their opinion, the <u>friendliness</u> between the writer and reader is maintained.

Dear Matt,
   It was great to hear from you in your last letter, although I can't help but disagree with what you say about travelling. I think the benefits of international travel far outweigh the costs!
   If you stick to holidays in the UK for your entire life, how will you ever learn about the different cultures in other countries? Sure, you might have fun on a holiday in Cornwall, doing the usual things us Brits do, but international travel broadens the mind, adds to your wealth of experience and heightens your awareness of the world around you.
   I know what you're thinking — that's all well and good, but it's cheaper to go on holiday in the UK, and you get similar benefits, too. Well, if you're not put off by the constant threat of drizzle, that may be the case. But I think it's worth spending a little bit more money (and with the rise of cheap flights, it is only a little bit) to avoid wasting your holidays hiding from the British rain.

Conversational style
This phrase would normally be used in a spoken conversation. This makes the reader feel like they are having a conversation with the writer, making the letter more <u>personal</u>.

Playful tone
The use of 'constant threat' to describe the rain is an example of hyperbole (exaggeration). This adds an element of humour to the letter, giving it a playful tone and creating a feeling of <u>warmth</u> between the writer and reader.

Yep, if there's one thing I know, it's style...

In the exam, as well as identifying the tone and style of a text, think about <u>why</u> they might have been used. One reason could be that the writer wants to make the reader feel certain emotions.

Tone and Style — Questions

Q1   Draw a line to match each sentence to the word that best describes its tone.

a) Forcing captive animals to perform tricks in zoos and circuses
is a repulsive and shameful practice that must not be tolerated!

b) Investigators have recently confirmed that DNA found at the
scene of the burglary matches that of suspect Fergus Maybach.

c) I had a riot helping out at the birthday party! Who would've
guessed that kids were the perfect audience for my magic tricks?

d) As he stared across the bay where they had first met, he remembered
vividly the tinkle of her laughter and the floral scent of her hair.

sentimental

detached

angry

upbeat

Q2   For each pair of sentences below, underline the sentence written in a formal style.

a) "Sorry! We don't take credit cards."
"Customers are advised that we do not accept credit cards."

b) "It is essential to ensure you have the correct tools before proceeding."
"Check you've got the proper kit to hand before you go any further."

c) "Rising debts? We've got the info you need to sort your finances out."
"If you have financial complications, contact our trained advisors."

Q3   The text below is taken from a travel journal.
Write down **three** pieces of evidence from the
text that show it has a conversational style.

*Gareth had always
been a style expert.*

> At this point I was starting to get a tad — how shall I put it? — cheesed
> off. It's one thing being patient, accepting the fact that things don't
> always go to plan and that now and then delays just happen. It's quite
> another to be told, after paying good money for a ticket to Town A, that
> for no good reason you're taking a little detour through Village B, River C
> and Swamp D. I was finding it more and more difficult to follow what I
> had figured was the local way of dealing with difficulties — smiling and
> pretending to find the grim industrial scenery interesting. It wasn't.

1) ....

2) ....

3) ....

Tone and Style — Questions

Now have a go at these exam-style questions — they will help you to put your knowledge into practice.

Q4 Read the following extract from a short story.

> Konrad Kaminski whistled as he ambled along the lane, twirling his umbrella as he went. It had been raining, but now the sun had burst through and was shining triumphantly. The puddles on the road glittered like molten silver, and the grass fields on either side offered up a heady scent of warm, wet earth. Everything radiated spring and promised summer.
>
> It was hard to tell if Konrad Kaminski was absorbing this positivity, or if he too was emitting it. Either way, his pink cheeks and sparkling eyes would have told a passer-by that here was a man for whom anything was possible. And indeed, had this been suggested to him, he would have agreed wholeheartedly. For here he was, a reasonably young man who had just come into a small fortune, and who had all the necessary intelligence and requisite enthusiasm to make that small fortune into a very large one.

How does the writer use language to create an upbeat tone?

You could include the writer's choice of:

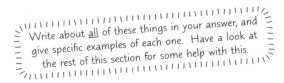

- words and phrases
- language features and techniques
- sentence forms.

Write about all of these things in your answer, and give specific examples of each one. Have a look at the rest of this section for some help with this.

Q5 Read the following extract from an adventure holiday brochure.

> If you're up to your neck in revision, the promise of a long summer holiday might be the only thing keeping you going. There's nothing wrong with wanting a break. You'll have earned it. Here at Adventure Action, we can give you the chance to do something unforgettable with your summer.
>
> If you're aged 15 to 18, you could spend four weeks on one of our incredible adventure and conservation programmes at breathtaking locations around the world. You could trek through dense rainforest in Peru to help build primary schools in isolated villages. You could take a flight over ancient glaciers to volunteer at a remote bear sanctuary in Alaska. Or you could earn a scuba-diving certificate whilst working in a marine biology lab in The Bahamas. Our programmes are tailored to give you a fantastic experience, where you can bag loads of new skills and be a part of something important.
>
> **Adventure beyond the usual this summer. Apply to Adventure Action today.**

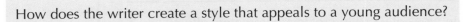

How does the writer create a style that appeals to a young audience?

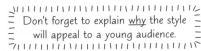
Don't forget to explain why the style will appeal to a young audience.

Think about what contributes to a text's style...

Lots of things make up the style of a text — language choices, sentence forms, structure... Try to think about how the style is built up from all of these different things when you're reading a text.

Words and Phrases

Writers choose certain words and phrases in order to create the effect they want.

Writers use a range of word types

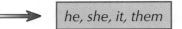
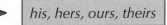

These pages will be really useful for paper 1, questions 2 and 4, and paper 2, questions 3 and 4.

It's helpful to be able to identify the <u>types</u> of words that a writer is using. Have a look at the <u>definitions</u> below to remind you:

1) <u>Nouns</u> are naming words — they refer to a person, place, thing or idea. ⟹ *sister, pen, art*

2) A <u>pronoun</u> is a word that can be used instead of a noun. ⟹ *he, she, it, them*

3) <u>Possessive pronouns</u> are pronouns that show ownership. ⟹ *his, hers, ours, theirs*

4) <u>Verbs</u> are doing words. ⟹ *think, run, swim, shout*

5) <u>Adjectives</u> describe a noun or pronoun. ⟹ *happy, clever, interesting*

6) <u>Adverbs</u> give extra information about verbs. ⟹ *quickly, loudly, accidentally*

Words and phrases can be used to achieve different effects

1) Words can <u>suggest</u> something <u>more</u> than their obvious meaning. For example:

> *Pedro <u>shut</u> the door.*
>
> *Pedro <u>slammed</u> the door.* ⟹ The verb 'slammed' has a similar meaning to 'shut', but it suggests that Pedro is <u>angry</u> or <u>tense</u>.

> *I <u>sniggered</u> when I saw Peter's costume.*
>
> *I <u>chuckled</u> when I saw Peter's costume.* ⟹ The verbs 'sniggered' and 'chuckled' both mean the writer <u>laughed</u>, but 'sniggered' suggests it in a nastier way — as if the writer is <u>making fun</u> of Peter.

2) Words can be chosen to achieve a specific <u>effect</u>. For example:

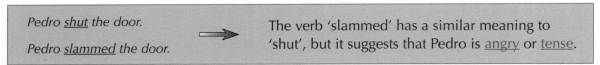

> *<u>my</u> dear reader*
>
> *<u>your</u> beloved pet* ⟹ Words like 'my', 'your' and 'our' help to create <u>familiarity</u> between the writer and the reader.

3) Writers might repeat certain <u>types</u> of word to create a <u>cumulative effect</u>. This just means that the <u>effect</u> of the words <u>builds up</u>. For example:

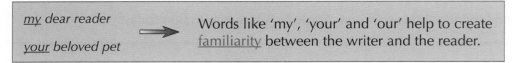

> Adjectives like 'electrifying', 'thrilling', 'tense' and 'intriguing' create a cumulative effect of excitement.

> The adverbs 'jovially', 'readily' and 'pleasantly combine to create an impression of enjoyment

Words and Phrases

Explain the effect of words and phrases

1) In the exams, you'll need to explain the <u>effect</u> of the writer's choice of <u>words and phrases</u>. Think about things like:

- What is <u>suggested</u> by the words and phrases <u>beyond</u> their obvious meaning.
- How the words and phrases might make the reader <u>feel</u>.
- How words and phrases affect the <u>tone</u> of the text.
- How the meaning of lots of words <u>builds up</u> to create an overall <u>effect</u>.

2) Have a look at the exam-style <u>text</u> below.

Adjectives
Effect: The adjectives 'magical', 'beautiful', 'balmy' and 'glistening' create an inviting cumulative effect. This gives the text a calming tone to make the reader feel <u>positive</u> about Bijoux Birthdays.

Phrase
Effect: The phrase 'a whole host' means the same as 'lots', but better emphasises that the number of acts to choose from is very large. This makes Bijoux Birthdays sound like a very <u>impressive</u> organisation.

A PICTURE-PERFECT PICNIC

Bijoux Birthdays invites you to celebrate your special day in style. Join us for a magical evening of entertainment on the beautiful banks of the River Fairer. Let us help you to relax in the balmy atmosphere of a warm summer's evening, recline next to the glistening waters and indulge in the most sumptuous of picnics.

We can tailor your evening to suit you. We can provide a refreshing feast for your senses. We can transport you to another place and time. Just sit back and let us do all the work. All you need to do is relax.

We have a large selection of menus for you to choose from, as well as a whole host of different entertainment acts — maybe you'd like a string quartet, or perhaps you'd be more interested in a circus act? Whatever your tastes, rest assured that we will be able to accommodate you.

If you're planning a celebration, Bijoux Birthdays really is the only choice.

Addressing the reader
Effect: Using 'you' and 'your' makes the reader feel as though the writer is speaking to them personally. This establishes <u>familiarity</u> with the reader.

Phrase
Effect: Repeating 'We can' creates a convincing cumulative effect. This emphasises that Bijoux Birthdays will give the reader an <u>enjoyable</u> experience.

Phrase
Effect: The phrase 'rest assured' <u>persuades</u> the reader that they can trust Bijoux Birthdays.

Words have power — sadly not the same kind as Superman...

When you read a text, think about the effect that the writer <u>wants</u> the whole text to have on the reader. Then you can consider how specific words and phrases help to achieve that effect.

Section Five — Reading: Use of Language

Words and Phrases — Questions

Q1 Write the words in the box into the correct columns in the table.

Remember, adjectives describe nouns or pronouns. Adverbs give extra information about verbs.

Adjectives	Adverbs
threatening	

~~threatening~~	phenomenal
boastfully	devotedly
lovely	bitterly

Q2 What does the word 'sneered' suggest in this sentence?

"Congratulations, Madge," Angus sneered.

....

....

Q3 How does the writer's choice of words create a different impression in each of the sentences below?

"Just go," she whispered.   *"Just go," she spat.*

....

....

....

Q4 Give **one** way that the author uses words and phrases to influence the reader in the sentence below.

As my dear friend, I am sure you will understand my decision.

....

....

Words and Phrases — Questions

If you're looking for some exam-style practice, then look no further than the questions below.

Q5   Read the following extract from a short story.

> The wind rose suddenly. It was a bitter wind, a stinging wind, a wind that drowned all thoughts in a roaring cacophony of noise and fury. It was a tempest that barged across the barren, open moorland and threw itself against the stone walls of the cottage. We didn't know when there would be an end to its howling or its persistent, unruly attempts to gain entry into our little home.
>
> We fought back the best we knew how, nailing boards against the window shutters to stop them being wrenched open by the gusts. Still it savaged us.
>
> "It can't get much worse, can it?" I asked Father, raising my voice above the roar of the enemy outside. His eyebrows drew together sternly.
>
> "We're just going to have to sit it out," he said.

When you're reading the text:
1. Underline the <u>words</u> and <u>phrases</u> that show the effects of the weather.
2. Think about the <u>effect</u> of these words and phrases on the <u>reader</u>.

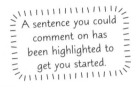
A sentence you could comment on has been highlighted to get you started.

How does the writer's choice of words and phrases show the effect of the weather?

Q6   Read the following extract from a piece of fiction.

> She raised an eyebrow at him icily. Her mouth was a stern, straight line.
> "Please," he pleaded, "it was a mistake. It won't happen again."
> Her silence was stone cold. He began to wring his hands fretfully. He could feel the sweat prickling like needles on the back of his neck. The seconds crawled by excruciatingly as he waited for her to say something, anything. He briefly considered speaking, but was too fearful of aggravating her further.
> "Evidently," she said at last, "you can no longer be trusted." The only emotion in her voice was disdain.
> His breath caught painfully in his chest; he knew the worst was coming.
> "I have no use for people I cannot trust," she continued. "You are dismissed. Leave now. Resign your post. Never let me see your face again. Understood?"
> Trembling, he managed a clumsy nod.
> "Good. Now get out."
> He turned and, dragging his feet like a condemned man, left the room.

How does the writer use words and phrases to present the characters in this passage?

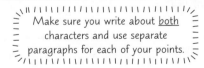
Make sure you write about <u>both</u> characters and use separate paragraphs for each of your points.

Explain why writers have chosen the words and phrases...

In the exam, make sure you explain <u>why</u> the writer has chosen the particular words and phrases that have been used. Don't just point out the word types used in the text without any explanation.

Section Five — Reading: Use of Language

Sentences

Sentences come in different types and lengths, which can be used to achieve different effects.

There are four main types of sentence

These pages will be really useful for paper 1, questions 2, 3 and 4, and paper 2, questions 3 and 4.

1) The four sentence types have different <u>purposes</u>.

2) <u>Statements</u> deliver <u>information</u>. For example:

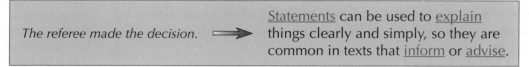

The referee made the decision. ⟹ <u>Statements</u> can be used to <u>explain</u> things clearly and simply, so they are common in texts that <u>inform</u> or <u>advise</u>.

3) <u>Questions</u> ask the reader something.

What would you do in my situation? ⟹ <u>Questions</u> don't always need an <u>answer</u> — they might be there to make the reader <u>think</u> about something.

4) <u>Commands</u> tell the reader to <u>do something</u>. They can also be called <u>orders</u>.

Consider the effects of this in the long term. ⟹ <u>Commands</u> might be used to <u>persuade</u> the reader to <u>do</u> or <u>think</u> something.

5) <u>Exclamations</u> show strong <u>emotions</u>.

This cannot be allowed to continue! ⟹ <u>Exclamations</u> help to <u>emphasise</u> the writer's <u>emotions</u>, and are common in <u>persuasive</u> texts.

6) For the <u>reading questions</u>, don't just <u>spot</u> the sentence types — comment on <u>why</u> writers have used them.

Writers use different sentence forms to interest the reader

1) Varying the <u>length</u> of sentences can create different <u>effects</u>.
    Here are a couple of <u>examples</u>:

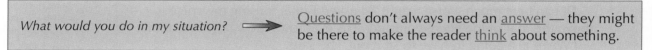

The sky was growing darker. I couldn't see where I was going. I stumbled. ⟹ Short sentences can be used to <u>build tension</u> or to create a <u>worried</u> and <u>confused</u> tone.

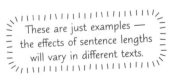

These are just examples — the effects of sentence lengths will vary in different texts.

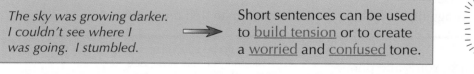

I waited excitedly at the foot of the stairs, listening to the footsteps above, thinking about the afternoon ahead, pacing the hall and counting down the minutes until we could set off. ⟹ A longer sentence could be used to give the impression of <u>time dragging</u>.

2) If you notice something about the way a writer has used sentences, don't just <u>identify</u> it. You need to comment on the <u>effects</u> to show how they <u>influence</u> the reader.

Sentences

Comment on why the sentence types and forms are used

1) You need to explain the <u>effect</u> of the sentence <u>types</u> and <u>forms</u> that you identify in the exam. You could think about things like:

- How the sentences help to achieve the writer's <u>purpose</u>.
- What the <u>effect</u> of the sentences on the <u>reader</u> might be.
- What <u>tone</u> the sentence types and forms help to create.
- What <u>style</u> the sentence types and forms help to create.

Tanya had adopted an alternative approach to determining sentence length.

© quintanilla/iStockphoto.com

2) Read the <u>text</u> below — you could get one like it in the <u>exam</u>.

Long sentence
Effect: This leaves the reader breathless by the end. It <u>highlights</u> the tiredness that the narrator is feeling.

Short sentence
Effect: This short sentence between two longer sentences <u>emphasises</u> the physical effects of the narrator's fear.

Short statement
Effect: This creates <u>anticipation</u> at the end of the text, leaving the reader wondering what will happen next.

It was late evening by the time I returned home from the shops, tired and weary from barging my way past all the desperate Christmas Eve shoppers. It had been a long day, and I was ready for a relaxing bath and a long sleep. It wasn't until I was halfway up the path that I noticed the front door was ajar. My heart began beating wildly inside my chest as I hesitantly advanced towards the door. My hands began to shake. My mind began conjuring apparitions of the unspeakable horrors that could be lurking inside. On reaching the door, I took a deep breath, collected my senses and stepped across the threshold. Everything was quiet and still. I crossed the hall and put down my shopping. Everything looked normal. Nothing was out of place. Suddenly I heard a noise above me. Someone was upstairs. I gasped. But then a change came over me: my fear had turned to resolute anger. Seldom had I experienced such intense fury in all my life. There was an intruder in my house, and they had no right to be there. I made for the stairs.

Short sentences
Effect: These short sentences build <u>tension</u>, making the reader share the narrator's feeling of dread.

Long sentence
Effect: This longer sentence marks a change in <u>tone</u> from fear to anger.

EXAM TIP

Short sentence. L o n g   s e n t e n c e.

If you're struggling to work out the effect of a sentence, imagine it being read out loud. If you think it sounds short and full of tension, it will probably have that effect on the reader, too.

Section Five — Reading: Use of Language

Sentences — Questions

Q1   The three sentences below say a similar thing in different ways.

a)
> *Bullying in schools is a serious problem.*

c)
> *We must stop bullying!*

b)
> *Haven't you had enough of bullying?*

| statement | exclamation | question |

For each sentence, identify the type of sentence using the options in the box.
Then explain why a writer might have chosen each one.

a) Sentence type: ....

....

....

b) Sentence type: ....

....

....

c) Sentence type: ....

....

....

Q2   Read the text below.

> Clutching the lottery ticket in my shaking hand, I sat inches away
> from the television, watching the screen eagerly as I waited for
> the last number to appear. The seconds seemed to stretch on for
> hours, days even, until it finally happened. Twenty-six. I'd won.

Give **one** way that the writer uses sentence length to create an effect.

....

....

....

Sentences — Questions

Commenting on sentence forms will get you marks in questions about both language and structure, so make sure you're prepared with these exam-style questions.

Q3 Read the following extract from a piece of fiction.

> The theatre hummed with expectant conversation as the spectators began to fill the stalls. There was a magical feeling, as if everyone knew they were going to witness something spectacular that night, and eyes kept flickering over to the theatre drapes, wondering when the show would begin.
>
> Backstage, biting his fingernails down to the nail-bed, was the one they were all waiting for. Mikhail had been told by everyone he met that he was the greatest tenor of all time. Conductors had shed a tear when he sang, audiences had wept openly. But that never stopped him from feeling sick with nerves before a performance. What if his voice faltered? What if he forgot the words? What if he disappointed them all?
>
> "Sixty seconds to curtain," the stage manager called to him. Mikhail took a deep breath. His palms were damp with sweat. His legs felt like jelly. He didn't know if he was ready for this.

When you're reading the text:

1. Underline any sentences that create <u>tension</u>.
2. Identify the features of each sentence — its <u>type</u> and whether it is <u>short</u> or <u>long</u>.
3. Think about <u>how</u> the features of each sentence create tension.

Don't forget to give examples to back up your points.

How has the writer used different sentence forms to create tension?

Q4 Read the following extract from a piece of fiction.

> The shot rang out. Jane powered off the blocks. Only one thing mattered now: putting one foot in front of the other, faster than she had ever done before. This was her race. She was born for this! Her blood pounded in her ears as she sprinted round the track.
>
> In the distance, the finish line was approaching. There were still two runners ahead of her. Faster! Jane urged herself on. Her legs burned. Her lungs screamed. But she was gaining on them. She overtook one. Still faster! At the last second, she overtook the final competitor and her foot came down first, landing triumphantly over the white line.
>
> Jane slowed to a halt, and doubled over with her hands on her knees. Gasping for breath, she looked up again at the stadium, and nearly cried with joy. Thousands and thousands of people were on their feet, cheering; they were waving flags and calling her name, smiles reaching from ear to ear. She could hardly believe it. All the months of hard training had paid off and she had achieved her lifelong dream: she had won a gold medal at the Olympics.

'Engage' just means 'interest'.

How has the writer used different sentence forms to engage the reader?

EXAM TIP

Discuss the effect of a sentence's type and form...

In the exam, write things like "this short exclamation creates the effect of..." or "the effect of this long question is..." to make sure you really explain the sentence features and their effects.

Section Five — Reading: Use of Language

Imagery

Imagery is where the writer uses different types of description to help the reader imagine something or understand an idea.

These pages will be useful for paper 1, questions 2 and 4, and paper 2, questions 3 and 4.

Metaphors and similes are comparisons

1) Metaphors and similes describe one thing by <u>comparing</u> it to something else.

| <u>Metaphors</u> describe something by saying that it <u>is</u> something else. | → | *His gaze <u>was</u> a laser beam, shooting straight through me.* |

| <u>Similes</u> describe something by saying that it's <u>like</u> something else. They use the words '<u>as</u>' or '<u>like</u>'. | → | *Walking through the bog was <u>like</u> wading through treacle.* |
| | → | *The wind was <u>as</u> cold <u>as</u> ice.* |

2) They help the reader to <u>imagine</u> what the writer is <u>describing</u>.

Similes made Jeremy feel as if the world had been turned upside down.

Analogies are also comparisons

1) Analogies are like <u>extended</u> similes — they compare one <u>idea</u> to another to make it easier for the reader to <u>understand</u>.

2) The idea is usually compared to something more <u>familiar</u> or more <u>shocking</u>. For example:

| *Deforestation is happening at an incredible speed. An area of rainforest as big as twenty football pitches is lost every minute.* | → | Comparing the area to something <u>familiar</u> like football pitches helps the reader to <u>understand</u> how much of the rainforest is being lost. |

Personification is describing a thing as a person

1) Personification is when a writer describes something as if it were a <u>person</u>.

2) This can make descriptions <u>more clear</u> and <u>powerful</u>:

| *The desk groaned under the weight of the books.* | → | The desk is described like a <u>person</u> struggling to carry something. This makes it <u>clear</u> to the reader that the books are very <u>heavy</u>. |

3) It can also show the <u>viewpoint</u> or <u>attitude</u> of the <u>writer</u> or <u>character</u>:

| *Military helicopters prowled the skies above the city.* | → | The helicopters are described as if they are <u>hunting</u> people. This shows that the writer feels that they are <u>threatening</u>. |

Imagery

Comment on why the writer has used the technique

1) In your <u>exam answers</u>, it's important to explain the <u>effects</u> of imagery, and <u>why</u> a writer has used it. Think about things like:

- How imagery might help the reader to <u>understand</u> or <u>imagine</u> something.
- How it might make the reader <u>feel</u>.
- How it might help the writer achieve their <u>purpose</u>.
- How it might affect the <u>tone</u> or <u>style</u> of the text.

2) Have a look at the <u>text</u> below — it's like one you'll get in the exam:

Simile
Effect: This helps the reader to <u>imagine</u> how uncomfortable and heavy the air felt.

Simile
Effect: Helps the reader to <u>understand</u> how the soldier was feeling — it was so frightening it didn't seem real.

The air clung to me like a warm, wet blanket. It was like living inside a horribly stifling nightmare. I just wanted to wake up, throw the blanket off the bed and breathe some cool, fresh air.

After a while, I couldn't tell what was nightmare and what wasn't. Once I was caught in an ambush, taking fire from three sides. The order came to fall back, and I found myself on my own, surrounded by bullets that hissed incessantly as they flew around, trying to sink their teeth into me. I tried to run, but my feet were blocks of concrete. I sat and cried, and hugged my weapon, a hard and hideous teddy bear for a terrified and broken man.

Far from fulfilling the exciting promise of 'making a difference' and 'seeing the world', being in the army had become like confronting all my worst tormentors at once, lined up with all their vicious hatred to conquer my will and break my spirit.

Metaphor
Effect: Helps the reader to <u>understand</u> the soldier's panic — he was so scared that he couldn't move.

Personification
Effect: The bullets are made to sound vicious and cruel. This makes the reader <u>sympathise</u> with the soldier's suffering.

Metaphor
Effect: Makes the reader <u>feel pity</u> for the soldier by showing that he needed comfort, but couldn't find any.

Analogy
Effect: This helps the reader to clearly understand the soldier's feelings towards the army. This might help to achieve the writer's <u>purpose</u> of showing the reader that being in the army is not as great as people may think.

I've got analogy to imagery...

When you read a text, think about what effect any imagery has on <u>you</u>. This will help you to put into words in your exam answers how the imagery might make the text's audience feel.

Imagery — Questions

Q1 Write 'S' next to the similes and 'M' next to the metaphors below.

a) She was a fraying cable of tension and anger, which could snap at any moment. ....

b) The lake was a mirror, reflecting the majesty of the sky above. ....

c) Like a flock of tired ducks, we clustered around our teacher,
who had brought us snacks to keep us going on the journey. ....

d) His eyes were hot coals, burning fiercely at the vision he saw before him. ....

e) The night sky was like a cloth of violet silk scattered with gemstones. ....

Q2 Read the texts below. How does the use of an analogy in the second text make it more effective?

> *A running tap wastes around 6 litres of water for every minute it's left running.*

> *A running tap wastes the equivalent of seventeen cups of tea for every minute it's left running.*

....

....

Q3 Underline **two** examples of personification in this advert,
then explain their effect on the reader on the lines below.

A Call for Heroic Hikers!

Are you a fearsome fell-runner? Or maybe you just enjoy long strolls through the hills? Whatever your ability, we want you to sign up for our 40-mile Wilderness Walk, taking place in the mountainous forest above Tennerton. If you train hard, you'll not only get fit, but triumph over a challenging foe and raise lots of money for charities in the local area. To answer the cry of the hills and get involved, visit the council's website.

© panorama/iStockphoto.com

Effect of first example: ....

....

Effect of second example: ....

....

Imagery — Questions

Here are some exam-style questions to help you practise explaining the effects of imagery.

Q4   Read the following extract from a piece of fiction.

> The landscape was dull steel. The sea, the sky and the mountains in the distance were all grey. And we were grey too. Our meagre rations of bread and nameless slop had left us sallow-faced, with dark rings under our eyes. We huddled together nervously, like mice in a cage. A thin layer of snow carpeted the tundra already. It was only September; plenty more snow would come. The cruel wind whipped at our cheeks and we shivered.
>
> The soldiers stood by the hut, spirals of smoke dancing upwards from the cigarettes they held aloft. They occasionally cast a sideways glance at us, making sure that we weren't doing anything foolish, like trying to escape. Eventually they trampled on their cigarettes and marched over to us — wolves in military uniform, coming to snarl at lambs.
>
> "There's work to do!" the officer in charge barked, clapping his gloved hands and then gesturing to the crates we'd unloaded. "Come on! Get a move on!" He fired his orders like cannon balls, and we dispersed frantically to do as he said. "If they're not all unpacked by nightfall, no one eats."

Some examples of these techniques have been highlighted to get you started.

How does the writer use metaphors, similes and personification to bring this scene to life for the reader?

Q5   Read the following extract from a leaflet about health.

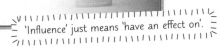

Driving towards a healthier you

If you had a Ferrari, I can only imagine that you would take good care of it. You might only fill its tank with premium fuel. You might have it regularly serviced. You would take pride in it, polish it at the weekends and keep the upholstery clean.

If you would take this much care of a Ferrari, surely you should take this much care of your body? After all, it's the only one you're ever going to have — you can't just trade this engine in if it breaks down. This means you should fuel yourself properly, eating regular meals that are full of the vitamins and minerals needed for optimum human performance. Keep your body's systems working effectively by exercising regularly. And finally, take pride in your body: if you're striving to be happy and healthy, that is something to celebrate.

Regardless of shape or size, your body is priceless — and that's more than you can say for a luxury sports car, isn't it?

'Influence' just means 'have an effect on'.

How does the writer use an analogy to try to influence the reader?

Prepare for the exam by learning definitions...

When it comes to imagery, there are a lot of definitions you need to know. To make sure you can definitely remember them, have a go at jotting them down without looking at page 52.

Language Sound Effects

Writers might use the sounds of words to capture the reader's attention or to help them imagine something.

Alliteration is the repetition of sounds

1) <u>Alliteration</u> is when words that are close together begin with the <u>same sound</u>.

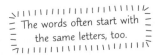
The words often start with the same letters, too.

2) It can have lots of different <u>effects</u>:

PM's <u>p</u>anic! ⟶	The <u>short</u> and <u>hard</u> 'P' sound captures the reader's attention by making the headline sound more <u>dramatic</u>. This might make the reader more <u>interested</u> in reading the article.

Try our new <u>S</u>uper <u>S</u>weeper today! ⟶	The <u>long</u> and <u>sharp</u> 'S' sound makes the name of the product sound more <u>striking</u>, so it is <u>memorable</u> to the reader.

The Lake District is a <u>h</u>eavenly <u>h</u>aven for <u>h</u>ill-walkers. ⟶	The <u>long</u> and <u>gentle</u> 'H' sound creates a calming <u>tone</u>, making the reader feel <u>positive</u> about the Lake District.

Onomatopoeia is when words imitate sounds

1) <u>Onomatopoeia</u> is when words <u>sound like</u> the noises they describe.

thud *crackle* *squish* *hiss* *smash* ⟶	These words imitate a <u>noise</u> when they are <u>spoken</u> aloud.

2) It helps the reader to <u>imagine</u> what the writer is describing:

We relaxed on the beach beside the <u>crackling</u> fire. ⟶	'Crackling' <u>sounds</u> like the noise that fire makes, so it helps the reader to <u>imagine</u> what the fire sounds like.

Suddenly, they stopped talking, and the only sound was the <u>tick tock</u> of the clock on the wall. ⟶	'Tick tock' <u>sounds</u> like the noise a clock makes. This helps the reader to clearly <u>imagine</u> the scene.

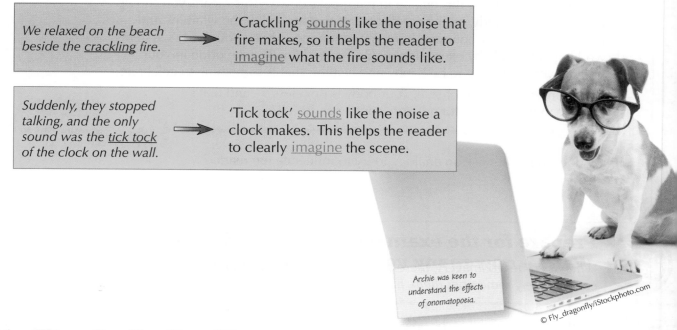
Archie was keen to understand the effects of onomatopoeia.

© Fly_dragonfly/iStockphoto.com

Language Sound Effects

Explain the effects of word sounds

1) Make sure you explain the <u>effect</u> alliteration and onomatopoeia have on the <u>reader</u>, and <u>why</u> they have that effect.
Think about:

> * What sounds are <u>imitated</u> by onomatopoeic words and how this helps the reader to <u>imagine</u> something.
> * What <u>effect</u> alliteration has (e.g. makes something more <u>dramatic</u>, <u>memorable</u> or <u>persuasive</u>).
> * How the <u>sounds</u> of the words <u>achieve</u> those effects.

2) Have a look at this <u>text</u> to see some of the <u>effects</u> of alliteration and onomatopoeia.

Alliteration
Effect: This grabs the reader's <u>attention</u> and makes them want to read the rest of the advert.

Alliteration
Effect: The repetition of the long, drawn out 'dr' sound emphasises the <u>boredom</u> associated with other drinks.

Alliteration
Effect: The repetition of the 'M' sound places emphasis on the 'magic' qualities of the product, making it sound more appealing and <u>impressive</u> to the reader.

MAKE MILKSHAKE MAGIC!

If you're bored with having the same old dreary drinks again and again, then it's time for you to shake it up with Milkshake Magic!

Just add our Milkshake Magic to a glass of milk, and listen to the powder fizz and crackle into a delicious drink that you'll be slurping up in no time!

Onomatopoeia
Effect: This helps the reader to imagine themselves drinking the product, which might <u>persuade</u> them to buy it.

Onomatopoeia
Effect: The words 'fizz' and 'crackle' help the reader to imagine what the product sounds like, which makes it seem more <u>exciting</u>.

Wait — how many vowels? No, that can't be right...

I know it's not fun, but you should really make sure you can spell <u>onomatopoeia</u>. You might need to write about it in the exam, so you may as well impress the examiner by spelling it correctly.

Language Sound Effects — Questions

Q1   Use the words in the box to complete the following sentences about language sound effects.

> attention   imagine   noise   memorable   repeated

Alliteration is when the sounds at the beginning of words are .... This has

many possible effects, such as capturing a reader's .... and making texts more

.... Onomatopoeia is when a word sounds like the ....

it describes. This can help a reader to .... something more clearly.

Q2   For each extract, circle the technique being used.
Then explain **one** effect that the technique creates.

a) "The buzz and chatter of the students ruined the tranquillity of the scene."

Alliteration / onomatopoeia

....

....

b) "Bag a Bargain at Brigson's — Portsmouth's Premier Pig Farm!"

Alliteration / onomatopoeia

....

....

Q3   Read the texts below. How does the use of onomatopoeia
in the second text make it a more effective description?

> *I could hear the animals
> beginning to surround us.*

> *The deep roars and rumbling growls told me
> that the animals were beginning to surround us.*

....

....

Language Sound Effects — Questions

And now, here's some handy exam-style practice for writing about these language techniques.

Q4   Read the following extract from a short story.

> It was dark in the forest, and eerily close. Even small sounds were amplified into threatening noises. They heard the sinister creaking of the branches; the furtive rustle of leaves; the cracking of a twig that set their hearts racing. And every time they looked behind them, they were sure the scene had changed. Had that fallen log been there before? Had they really not seen that stream? It was as if the forest was playing tricks on them — purposefully trying to deceive and confuse them. Shadows seemed to shift, skipping about the forest floor, delighted at the predicament of the lost wanderers.
>
> Suddenly they heard a shrill screech. It pierced their ears and stopped them dead. The noise rang out again and they squinted upwards to see a large but haggard owl perching on a branch, staring down threateningly. It was guarding the path ahead.

In your answer:
1. Make <u>points</u> to answer the question.
2. Give <u>examples</u> of onomatopoeia to support your points.
3. <u>Explain</u> how the examples <u>support</u> your points.
4. Explain the <u>effect</u> of the examples.

Some examples of onomatopoeia have been highlighted to get you started.

How does the writer use onomatopoeia to describe this scene?

Q5   Read the following extract from a piece of travel writing.

> The streets of Kuala Lumpur are a labyrinth of lost lanes, back-streets, dead-ends and alleys, which twist and turn and double back on themselves, constantly trying to bewilder the unaccustomed traveller. An apparently infinite series of haphazard side streets break out from the main street of the Chinatown area, like snakes winding across the desert. Heavy trucks rumble past impatiently, whilst thousands of scooters whine and buzz like a swarm of bees, honking horns and hurling out exhaust fumes that stubbornly stagnate in the desperately hot air. The heat is relentless. Even standing still in the shade I can feel the sweat gathering on my forehead.
>
> In search of an escape from the choking fumes, I make my way to the city centre park. Here, neat pathways wind their way leisurely through immaculate green lawns. A soothing tinkling and splashing sound drifts over from a water fountain nearby. On every side of the park, glimmering steel skyscrapers tower into the sky, peering down at the people below. It's like being surrounded by a giant metal rainforest, thronging with life.

Remember to use separate <u>paragraphs</u> for each of your points.

How does the writer use alliteration and onomatopoeia to convey their attitude to Kuala Lumpur?

Imagine the sounds made by the words...

When you come across examples of alliteration and onomatopoeia, it might be helpful for you to imagine them being read <u>aloud</u> — so you can put a finger on what the effects of the <u>sounds</u> are.

Section Five — Reading: Use of Language

Rhetoric

Rhetorical techniques are used to make language more persuasive. This page will show you how...

Rhetorical questions make the reader think

1) <u>Rhetorical questions</u> are questions that don't need an <u>answer</u>.

2) They make the reader <u>think</u> about the answer they might give, but the writer often <u>phrases</u> the question so there is only one <u>sensible</u> answer.

3) This makes the reader feel like they've made their <u>own</u> mind up, but actually the writer is trying to <u>persuade</u> them about something. For example:

> *Is it right that footballers are paid such vast sums of money?* The question is written so that the only sensible <u>answer</u> is 'no'. This <u>persuades</u> the reader that footballers are paid too much.

Hyperbole is exaggeration

1) <u>Hyperbole</u> is when a writer deliberately <u>exaggerates</u> something.

2) It is used to make a point very <u>clearly</u> and <u>forcefully</u>. For example:

> *We had to wait <u>forever</u> for the food to arrive.* They didn't actually have to wait '<u>forever</u>', but the effect is to <u>stress</u> that they had to wait a long time.

Bobby had said a million times that he hated checkered shirts.

Lists and repetition emphasise a point

1) Writers often use a <u>list of three</u> words or phrases to <u>emphasise</u> the point they're making. They often list three <u>adjectives</u>, for example:

> *The cross-country run is <u>painful</u>, <u>pointless</u> and pure <u>evil</u>.* Using a <u>list of three</u> adjectives emphasises the writer's strong <u>negative feelings</u> towards the run. This might <u>persuade</u> the reader to <u>agree</u> with the writer's opinion.

2) Writers might also <u>repeat</u> the <u>same word</u> or <u>phrase</u> to emphasise a point.

> *People who exercise regularly are <u>more likely</u> to be happy, <u>more likely</u> to be healthy and <u>more likely</u> to live longer.* The <u>repetition</u> of 'more likely' emphasises the writer's belief in the <u>importance</u> of regular exercise. This could <u>persuade</u> the reader to try to exercise more <u>often</u>.

Rhetoric

Point out the effects of rhetorical techniques

1) As well as identifying <u>examples</u> of rhetorical techniques, explaining their <u>effects</u> is <u>essential</u>. Here are a few things you might think about:

- How they might <u>persuade</u> a reader to think or do something.
- How they might make a reader <u>feel</u>.
- How rhetorical techniques might show a writer's <u>attitude</u>.
- What <u>tone</u> and <u>style</u> are created by rhetorical techniques.

2) Look at the <u>text</u> below:

Rhetorical question
Effect: The question is phrased so that the only sensible answer is 'no'. This could <u>persuade</u> the reader to think that it is unfair for students to receive more homework.

List of three adjectives
Effect: This emphasises the writer's negative feelings towards being given more homework. This could <u>persuade</u> the reader to agree that it is unfair.

List of three phrases
Effect: This highlights the amount of work that students already do. This might <u>persuade</u> the reader that students don't need any more homework.

Hyperbole
Effect: Students don't literally study 'every hour', but this emphasises the large amount of time they do spend working. This might <u>persuade</u> the reader that students shouldn't be given more homework.

Repetition
Effect: The writer repeatedly tells the reader, 'Join me', which could have the effect of <u>persuading</u> the reader to join the campaign.

Rhetorical question
Effect: This is written in a way that suggests to the reader that students will have no time to enjoy themselves if they receive more homework. This could <u>persuade</u> the reader to think students shouldn't be given more homework.

> This plan to give students across the country more homework is disgusting, inconsiderate and cruel.
>
> Can it really be fair to set us even more ridiculous and unnecessary assignments? It's as if they don't think we work every hour of the day already! We are expected to study all day in the classroom, take part in extracurricular activities, then do homework during evenings and weekends. This plan will only add to our already backbreaking workloads.
>
> Of course, no one can deny that studying is important. However, time reserved for rest and relaxation is just as essential. If this plan goes ahead, when will we have time for our own hobbies and interests? More homework will only serve to erase any fulfilment we might get from our lives outside of school.
>
> Join me if you're interested in a better work/life balance. Join me to make our voices heard. Join me in my campaign for less homework!

Revision is a fun, exciting, thrilling way to spend an evening...

In your exam answers, write about exactly how rhetorical techniques will persuade a reader.
For example, it might be by making them feel certain emotions, such as sympathy or excitement.

Rhetoric — Questions

Q1   Draw lines to match each sentence to its technique.

a) Who would want to eat a sandwich covered in mould?

b) The sandwich was old, mouldy and disgusting.

c) Nothing is more disgusting than a mouldy sandwich.

list of three

rhetorical question

hyperbole

Q2   Underline **three** rhetorical techniques in this passage. Then on the
lines below, name the technique and explain the effect on the reader.

> *Who has not felt outraged at the injustice of the world when viewing
> images of child poverty? We live in a world where millions of children
> must battle with hunger, thirst and poor sanitation every day. Your
> donation can make a difference. Your donation can eradicate poverty.
> Your donation will truly change these children's lives for the better.*

Technique: ....

Effect: ....

....

....

Technique: ....

Effect: ....

....

....

Technique: ....

Effect: ....

....

....

Rhetoric — Questions

If you need to write about rhetoric in your exam, these exam-style questions will help you prepare.

Q3   Read the following extract from a travel brochure.

> Do you ever dream of turning your back on the daily drudge and escaping on a luxury break? Well, look no further than Malliwest Holidays — offering the best range of exclusive package holidays for the discerning traveller.
>
> Perhaps your perfect escape features breathtaking Arctic scenery? If so, let us take you on an adventure to Iceland. Here you can be astounded by the Northern Lights, the world-famous volcanic hot springs and our expertly guided whale-watching tours.
>
> Or perhaps your idea of adventure is a five-star African safari? Malliwest's safari camps in Kenya offer lavish accommodation and the services of expert wildlife rangers, who will bring you face to face with animals such as lions, zebra and gazelle.
>
> And if relaxation is what you need, then rest assured that our top-end, all-inclusive beach resorts will satisfy your every desire. Your every wish will be catered for by our dedicated, professional staff.
>
> We can't wait to welcome you on your well-deserved break.

For each point you make:
1. State what the writer is trying to <u>persuade</u> the reader to <u>think</u> or <u>do</u>.
2. Say what <u>rhetorical technique</u> the writer uses to do this, and give an <u>example</u>.
3. Explain <u>how</u> it persuades the reader, including what <u>effect</u> it has.

How does the writer use rhetorical techniques to try to persuade the reader?

Underline the <u>keywords</u> in the question so you know what you are expected to do.

Q4   Read the following extract from a review posted on a travel website.

> Upon entering the hotel and approaching the reception desk, we were met by a rude, unhelpful and completely unprofessional member of staff. We waited patiently while he finished his conversation with his friends before he eventually noticed us and greeted us with a grunt. He then provided some baffling directions around the hotel, threw a keycard at us and sent us off to find our room alone. Would it really have been asking too much for him to give us a hand with the suitcases?
>
> After spending an age wandering hopelessly around the hotel, we eventually found our room. Unfortunately, it was here where the horror really started: based on the overpowering smell of damp, I can only assume that the window hadn't been opened for about a century. The wallpaper was stained, the carpet was stained and the bedding was stained. And the thought of sleeping on the paper-thin mattress almost brought me to tears.

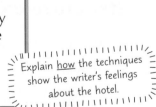

Explain <u>how</u> the techniques show the writer's feelings about the hotel.

How does the writer use rhetorical techniques to convey their attitude to the hotel?

Discuss other persuasive techniques that writers use...

There are other ways that writers might persuade their readers. One way might be through their choice of words and phrases. See pages 44-45 for more about the effects of words and phrases.

Section Six — Reading: Structure

Structure

This section is about structure — the way texts are organised. Structure is especially important for paper 1, question 3. You might also write about it in question 4 on both papers.

Fiction uses structure to entertain and interest the reader

1) <u>Structure</u> is the way a writer <u>organises</u> their <u>ideas</u> in a text.

2) In <u>fiction</u> writing, writers might use different structures to have different <u>effects</u>.

3) They can use a <u>linear structure</u>, where the events of a <u>whole text</u> are arranged in <u>time order</u>. This can make the text <u>easy to follow</u>.

4) They might also use a <u>non-linear structure</u> — that's when the events of a story happen <u>out of time order</u>.

> *... I was sick of stuffy classrooms and the endless squeak of chalk against the blackboard.*
> *<u>The week before</u>, we'd rebelled, taking our chairs outside and learning under the clear blue sky...*

This text includes a <u>flashback</u>. It allows the writer to write about an event that happened in the <u>past</u>.

5) A text might have <u>more than one</u> narrator, or <u>move</u> between different characters' <u>viewpoints</u>.

> *... <u>Georgia</u> was incredibly <u>nervous</u>.*
> *Across the room, <u>Anisha</u> was <u>thrilled</u>. Her favourite topic had come up on the test!*

This text has <u>two</u> viewpoints in it. This helps the reader to <u>understand</u> two <u>separate</u> characters better.

6) The <u>start</u> and <u>end</u> of a text are important to its structure.

> *Thomas banged frantically against the metal door. They had twelve minutes to escape the building, and he knew that they weren't going to make it.*

This is the <u>start</u> of a longer text. It begins in the <u>middle</u> of the action, which helps to <u>draw the reader in</u>.

> *They walked away, certain that Captain Greymane had gone down with his ship. They did not see the dark shape slowly dragging itself out of the water on to the rocks below.*

This is the <u>ending</u> of a longer text. It finishes on a <u>cliffhanger</u>, which is <u>interesting</u> and <u>exciting</u> for the reader.

Structure can be used to direct the reader's attention

A writer will often use <u>structural techniques</u> to <u>guide</u> the reader through a text. For example:

1) They might <u>describe</u> something <u>general</u>, then <u>narrow</u> down to something <u>specific</u>.

> *I gazed across the broad valley, taking in the vast blanket of green fields. As I looked, I found myself focusing on one field in particular.*

This describes the valley, then <u>focuses</u> on a field, which helps to create a <u>detailed scene</u>.

2) They could <u>describe</u> a <u>journey</u>.

> *The train moved silently from village to village, stopping for a few minutes at each identical station before gliding on into the night.*

The narrator <u>describes</u> the journey, to make the reader feel like they're <u>travelling too</u>.

Structure

Paragraphs and sentences create structure too

1) You need to write about <u>more</u> than just the structure of the <u>whole text</u>.

2) Think about how <u>paragraphs</u> are used to structure the text. For example:

> <u>New paragraphs</u> show that the writer is going to talk about a new <u>topic</u>, a different <u>character</u>, or a different <u>time</u> or <u>place</u>.

> A writer might put a <u>single sentence</u> into its <u>own paragraph</u> to show that it's <u>important</u>.

> Lots of <u>short paragraphs</u> can make it seem like a story is moving very <u>fast</u>.

> A <u>long paragraph</u> could be used to <u>slow</u> a story down.

3) Individual <u>sentences</u> can also be used to structure the text:

- <u>Long sentences</u> might be used to make the reader <u>wait</u> to find something out.
- <u>Short sentences</u> can be used to <u>shock</u> the reader, or break up the <u>flow</u> of a text.

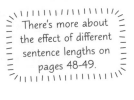
There's more about the effect of different sentence lengths on pages 48-49.

Structure can help to achieve the writer's purpose

In <u>non-fiction</u> writing, structure can be used to help the writer achieve their <u>purpose</u>.

- When writing to <u>advise</u>, a writer might put instructions in an <u>order</u> that's <u>easy to follow</u>.

- When writing to <u>persuade</u>, a writer might use <u>repetition</u> to <u>emphasise</u> important points.

- When writing to <u>argue</u>, a writer might include an <u>introduction</u> and a <u>conclusion</u>, to make their argument very <u>clear</u>.

- When writing to <u>inform</u>, a writer might use <u>paragraphs</u> to break up the information in a text, which makes it easier for the reader to <u>understand</u>.

© Kobyakov/iStockphoto.com

Charlie took the structure of his text very seriously.

KEY SKILL

This book is structured so that you ace your exams...

Structure plays a huge part in every text you read, so you'll need to really get to grips with the way that it works. There's an example text on the next two pages to help you get started with that.

Structure

Write about the effect of the text's structure

1) When you write about <u>structural features</u> in your exam,
   you need to write about <u>what</u> effect each feature has.
   Here are a few things you could think about:

   - How the structure is <u>suitable</u> for the <u>audience</u> and <u>purpose</u> of the text.
   - How the structure affects the overall <u>tone</u> and <u>style</u> of the text.
   - The <u>effect</u> that the structural features have on the <u>reader</u>.

2) On this page and the next, there's an extract from an <u>exam-style text</u> for you to look at:

General description that narrows down
Effect: This creates a <u>detailed scene</u>, gradually drawing the reader <u>into the story</u>.

Guided description
Effect: The path is used to <u>guide</u> the reader through the description of the scene.

   The mountain looked a little mysterious in the half-light of the dusky evening. Its snow-capped peak stood alert, bathing in the dying embers of the setting sun. From there, my eye was drawn to the narrow path that wound its way precariously down past the dark woods and craggy outcrops of the mountain face. I traced the weaving path all the way down, until it vanished behind the spire of a magnificent church that loomed over the town nestled at the foot of the mountain.

Repetition
Effect: This tells the reader that the town is <u>important</u> to the narrator.

   This was the town of my youth.
   This was the town where I had taken my first steps. This was the town where I had been to school, where I had battled through those tough transition years of teenage angst and, finally, where I had first fallen in love. It was permeated with memories of childhood games and, later in my adolescence, secret late-night trysts.

Describing a journey
Effect: Makes the reader feel like they're on the <u>same journey</u> as the narrator, so they can clearly imagine what the narrator is experiencing.

   I crossed the road and entered the alley that would take me deeper into the warren of streets that wound their way around the foot of the imposing church. When I finally emerged into the square, I was assaulted by a barrage of sights and smells that instantly took me all the way back to my youth.

The text continues on the next page.

Topic change
Effect: Smoothly introduces the <u>flashback</u> in the next paragraph.

Structure

Non-linear structure
Effect: Allows the narrator to tell a story from their <u>past</u>, which helps the reader to understand the character and the story better.

Immediately, I was back under the oak tree, crouching silently next to my best friend Sally. We were hiding from James Cotton, and it was matter of grave honour that we preserved our hiding place.

Back then, a game of hide and seek was no mere playground triviality. It was a fierce battle between the sexes, a passionately fought war between two equally resolute forces. We spent endless days squirrelled away in the nooks and crannies of the town we knew like the back of our hand, listening out warily for the tell-tale scramble of footsteps that meant James had found our hiding place.

Long sentence
Effect: Emphasises the 'endless days' of the narrator's childhood.

Use of paragraphs
Effect: <u>Paragraphs</u> are used here to help the reader follow both the narrator's <u>thoughts</u> and her <u>journey</u>. They show changes in topic, time, character or place.

Both Sally and I were fascinated with James: he was old for his age, smart and funny. Obviously, at that age, this fascination manifested itself as bitter hatred. For me, the coyness would come later, at around the same time as the feelings of claustrophobia and a strong yearning for the big city. Sally hadn't felt the same longing for the metropolis as I had, but she had discovered the coyness that would replace the naive and innocent feud. She had stayed here and built a life for herself.

Tomorrow morning I was to attend the wedding at which she would become Mrs Cotton.

One-sentence paragraph
Effect: This suggests that the wedding is going to be an <u>important</u> event in the story.

The tolling of the church bells brought me back to the present with a start. I needed to hurry if I was to get to my parents' house before dinnertime. With a sigh of nostalgia, I turned away from the old oak tree, and began the final leg of the journey back to my former home...

Overall structure
Effect: The <u>overall structure</u> of the text takes the reader along with the narrator on her <u>journey</u> through the town. The writer also uses this journey to take the reader on a <u>second journey</u> through the <u>narrator's childhood</u>.

This is the end of an <u>extract</u>, but it's not the end of the <u>whole text</u>. Make sure you don't get confused between these two things in your exam.

The bride was fairly confident that the guests would be able to spot the wedding venue.

Draw your attention? But I've left my crayons at home...

In questions about structure, think about how the writer is using structure to direct your attention. Don't forget to write about paragraph- and sentence-level features, as well as the whole text.

Structure — Questions

Q1 Draw lines to match each structural technique with its definition.

a) **Non-linear writing**

b) **Linear writing**

i) Writing that tells the events of a story in time order.

ii) Writing that doesn't tell the events of a story in time order.

Proof that structure is important.

Q2 Read the extract below.

> It was one of those frosty winter mornings. The sky was a clear forget-me-not blue, and the grass stood rigid and silver with frost. Robins chirped proudly as they flittered in and out of the glittering bramble bushes. The kitchen sang with the smell of hot, buttered toast and fried bacon. A large, red pot of tea sat on the kitchen table, steam curling from its spout.

Cross out the incorrect word from each pair of bold words.

a) This extract opens with **description / speech**.

b) This means that the reader's focus is initially on the **setting / characters**.

c) It moves the reader's attention from **outside / inside** to **outside / inside**.

Q3 Choose **one** structural feature from the extract below. On the lines underneath, explain the effect that it has on the reader.

> I surveyed the chaos of Alice's usually pristine bedroom for a moment, astounded by the mess of abandoned takeaway cartons and tear-stained tissues. Then I focused my attention on Alice, who blew her nose before looking up at me through red-rimmed eyes.
> "I'll tell you what happened," she said, and took a breath. "It all started last week, when Robyn and I came out of the cinema. We bumped into Hayley and Dan, and we all decided to go for dinner to that new burrito bar that's opened in town..."

Feature: ....

Effect: ....

....

....

Structure — Questions

Try this exam practice question, then use the boxes at the bottom to mark how well you think you did.

Q4 This is the ending to a short story. Joan is eighty-six years old, and one of the nurses from her care home has volunteered to take her to the beach.

> They arrived shortly before lunchtime. The seagulls squawked noisily overhead, swooping and circling, bright as doves against the blue sky. The nurse pushed the wheelchair down the boardwalk, the wheels clattering merrily against the wooden surface.
>
> Looking out over the sand and the grey-green sea, Joan was completely transfixed.
>
> The first time she had been to the beach was as a little girl, shortly before the war broke out. It had been a hot day. The beach was full of people sprawled on multicoloured deck-chairs and picnic blankets, lending the scene a carnival feel. Her mother had packed a picnic of hard-boiled eggs and potato salad, and they had bought ice-cream cones from a man wheeling a wooden cart. She remembered the smell of the water as she raced into the sea for the first time. She remembered the feeling of damp sand between her fingers and toes, and how the sea salt had dried into tiny crystals on her skin. It had been the best day of her life so far, and as her father had bundled her into a towel, tired and sun-soaked, ready to go home, she had already been looking forward to the next visit.
>
> Now Joan watched the children race delightedly across the sand as she had done. Her nurse bought her fish and chips for lunch. Joan bought sticks of garishly coloured rock for her great-grandchildren. As the sun began to sink, and they headed back to the car, Joan looked back over her shoulder. She knew there wouldn't be a next visit — but she didn't mind. She had seen the sea again.

Helpful tips:
1. Use <u>examples</u> from the text to support your points. (Remember, these <u>don't</u> have to be direct quotes.)
2. <u>Explain</u> how your examples support your points — say <u>how</u> they make the text more <u>interesting</u>.
3. Try to focus your answer on the <u>effect</u> of each structural feature — how it keeps the <u>reader</u> interested in the text.

How has the writer structured the text to interest you as a reader?

You could write about:
- what the writer focuses your attention on at the beginning
- how and why the writer changes this focus as the extract develops
- any other structural features that interest you.

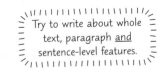
Try to write about whole text, paragraph <u>and</u> sentence-level features.

Focus your answers on the effect of the structure...

Write about the effect that each structural feature has on the reader. Non-fiction is often structured to make its content clear, or to be persuasive. Fiction is usually structured to interest the reader.

Section Seven — Writing: Creative Texts

Writing Creatively — Stories

Story-writing is a task that might come up in paper 1, question 5. You might have to write a short story, or a part of a longer story, like the opening or the ending.

Grab your reader's attention from the start

Avoid openings that are used a lot, like 'Once upon a time'.

Start your stories with an opening sentence that will make your reader want to carry on reading. For example, you could start a story in the middle of the action:

I couldn't believe it. He was gone. "He must be here," I thought as I desperately searched the shed. It was no use. Peter had run away, and it was all my fault.	This creates an exciting opening to the story, so the reader will want to keep reading to find out what happens next.

Use interesting language and structure in your stories

1) Different word choices have different effects.

2) Using varied vocabulary will make your story more entertaining to read. For example:

I glanced at Verity, who grinned furtively across the room.	The verbs 'glanced' and 'grinned' are more interesting than other verbs, such as 'looked' and 'smiled'. The adverb 'furtively' is also more descriptive than a word such as 'secretively'.

3) Organise your writing into paragraphs, and try to structure your writing in an interesting way. For example, you could use a non-linear structure with features such as flashbacks.

4) Use different sentence lengths to create effects. For example:

See pages 64-67 for more about structure.

The timer reached zero. That was it. It was over.	These abrupt, short sentences help to create a tense atmosphere, which makes the text more exciting for the reader.

It's important to write a good ending

You also need to finish your writing well. Here are some ways you could end a piece of story writing:

- You could finish with an unexpected plot twist that will shock the reader.

- You could show the main character coming to some kind of realisation.

- You could create a cliffhanger ending by finishing with a question. This will leave the reader thinking about what will happen next.

- You could have a neat, happy ending that will satisfy the reader.

Buster had come to the realisation that he was going to need a hair cut.

Writing Creatively — Stories

Always aim to entertain the reader

1) Whether you are asked to write a <u>short story</u> or <u>part</u> of a story, it should be <u>interesting</u> to the reader all the way through.

2) Here are a few things you can do to pick up <u>marks</u>:

- Write <u>about</u> something interesting and use creative <u>vocabulary</u>.
- Make sure your writing is <u>well-organised</u>, with an interesting <u>structure</u>.
- Write <u>accurately</u>, with good spelling, punctuation and grammar.

3) Have a look at this answer to an <u>exam-style</u> question:

PAPER 1

| 0 | 5 |

You are going to enter a creative writing competition run by your local book shop. The competition is being judged by the staff in the shop.

Write the ending of a story about somebody who made a bad decision.

Interesting opening
The narrator has come to a <u>realisation</u>, which hints to the reader that the story is about to come to an end.

Clear structure
This writing is organised into <u>paragraphs</u>. The first paragraph outlines the narrator's bad decision. The second paragraph shows what the narrator did next. Finally, the third paragraph shows the outcome of the decision.

Interesting vocabulary
The word 'scoured' is much more <u>interesting</u> than 'looked round', as it suggests how desperately and closely the narrator looked.

> I knew I should never have stolen the vase. It had been a moment of madness. I had just seen it sitting there, and it looked so beautiful and elegant. All of my problems started after that decision, that single flash of foolishness.
> I spent a long time wondering what to do with the vase. I studied it intently. It was too beautiful to discard, too dazzling to keep concealed any longer. Eventually, I made a decision.
> I took it to the cliff and threw it over, watching it smash on the rocks below. It was an awful sight, but at least my guilty secret was gone forever.
> Late that night, the wind was howling around my tent, and the rain was pelting down on the canvas. Suddenly, there was a huge crash of thunder and a blinding flash of lightning. Terrified, I ran out of the tent, only to be greeted by a strange sight: there, sitting on top of a tree stump, was the missing vase. It was completely whole. Not a single crack was visible on its smooth, shiny exterior. I whirled around and scoured the field for any sign of an intruder. That was when I saw the old, hunched man walking slowly away.

Sentence lengths
Two short sentences are used, with a longer sentence in between them. This helps to show the narrator's worry about what to do, and builds <u>tension</u> towards the end of the story.

Plot twist
An unexpected event can <u>surprise</u> the reader and make them feel excited about the story.

Dramatic ending
This <u>interests</u> the reader, as they are left with a feeling of curiosity about the old man.

EXAM TIP

"It was all a dream" — the examiner's nightmare...

Seriously, don't use this ending — the examiner will think you haven't put any thought into your story. If you are running out of time at the end, finish your story in a way that's short but effective.

Writing Creatively — Descriptions

For paper 1, question 5 you could be asked to write a description.
Your aim is to give your audience a detailed idea about a character or scene.

Descriptions show what something or someone is like

1) Descriptions create an <u>impression</u> of a person or place for the reader.

2) You <u>don't</u> need to include too much <u>action</u> — focus on <u>describing</u> the subject.

3) Descriptions need <u>detail</u>. For example, a <u>character</u> description might include:

- A character's <u>physical features</u>, e.g. hair colour, clothing.
- A character's <u>personality</u>, e.g. they could be funny, serious, quiet, sociable.
- Any other <u>features</u> that show <u>more</u> about them, e.g. any nervous habits.
- Your <u>opinion</u>, e.g. what you like or dislike about them.

Martin had some difficulty describing Alex's hair colour.

Descriptions should entertain the reader

\\|||||||||||||||||||||||/
See section 5 for more about
the effects of language choices
and language techniques.
/|||||||||||||||||||||||\\

1) You can make your descriptions <u>interesting</u> by using <u>creative language</u>:

The old locket was very delicate. *The ancient locket was as delicate as a butterfly's wing in the palm of my hand.*	The <u>second</u> description uses the more interesting <u>adjective</u> 'ancient' instead of 'old'. It also uses the <u>simile</u> 'as delicate as a butterfly's wing' to <u>show</u> that the locket is very delicate.

2) You can also use different <u>senses</u> to make a description interesting and bring a scene to <u>life</u>.
You could say what something <u>sounds</u> like:

The stream <u>babbled</u> softly outside my window.	<u>Onomatopoeia</u> is used to help the reader imagine what the stream <u>sounds</u> like.

You could also say what something <u>feels</u> like:

The sand was scorching against my feet.	'Scorching' shows that the sand <u>feels</u> extremely hot.

You might also describe what something <u>smells</u> or <u>tastes</u> like:

When I entered the house, the familiar smell of baked scones filled my nostrils.	This helps the reader to <u>imagine</u> the comforting <u>smell</u> in the house.

3) You should <u>structure</u> your descriptions so that they are <u>interesting</u> to read. For example:

The room was enormous and cluttered: spindly-legged tables were scattered around it, each one adorned with several tiny, intricate ornaments.	This starts by giving a <u>general</u> description of the room. It then goes on to describe some more <u>specific</u> details.

Writing Creatively — Descriptions

Create a mental picture with descriptions

1) Descriptions should help the <u>reader</u> to clearly <u>picture</u> what you're writing about. Here are some things you could do to make your descriptions really <u>effective</u>:

- Use interesting <u>language</u> to make your descriptions <u>entertaining</u> for the reader.
- Use <u>language techniques</u> (e.g. similes, metaphors) to create <u>vivid</u> descriptions.
- <u>Structure</u> your descriptions to make them <u>interesting</u> for the reader.

2) Have a look at this answer to an exam-style <u>description</u> question:

PAPER 1

| 0 | 5 |

You are going to enter a writing competition run by your school newspaper. The competition is being judged by your headteacher.

Write a description featuring this character:

© MarcusPhoto1/iStockphoto.com

Character's habits
Describing the woman's habits helps to give the reader an idea of her personality.

> The woman's fingernails tapped impatiently against the wood of the mantelpiece. She was standing still, but the motion of her perfectly-manicured fingernails, and the impatient huffs of air that were regularly expelled from between her thin lips, made her seem restless and agitated. Somehow she gave the impression that she never really stopped moving.

Structure
The description starts with a tiny detail, then expands outwards. This helps to give the writing an effective <u>structure</u>.

> She was an angular exclamation mark of a woman, and she stuck out like a sore thumb against our familiar, homely surroundings. She wore her dark hair in a short, businesslike style,

Metaphor
Using imagery makes the description more <u>interesting</u> to read.

> giving the impression that she was a woman to be taken seriously. Her suit was an inky black colour, which only served to emphasise her militantly slender form. When she spoke, her voice was low and commanding, and her expression was set into a permanent frown that was half-angry, half-distracted, and wholly intimidating.

Senses
Saying what the woman sounds like adds <u>detail</u>, making the description more <u>vivid</u>.

> She was the most terrifying person I had ever met.

Narrator's viewpoint
This shows the effect that the woman has on other people, which helps the reader to <u>understand</u> that she is very intimidating.

KEY SKILL

Use a range of different language techniques...

Try not to overuse any one technique — aim to use a variety of methods in your descriptions, including interesting adjectives and verbs, similes, metaphors, hyperbole and onomatopoeia.

Writing Creatively — Questions

Q1   Imagine you are going to write a short story about somebody who's lost in a forest.

    a) Write down two descriptive adjectives you could use in the story, and explain their effect.

    ....

    ....

    b) Write an interesting opening sentence for the story.

    ....

    ....

    c) Write the closing sentences of the story.

    ....

    ....

Q2   Write a description to match each of the following requirements.

    a) Use personification to describe an old car.

    ....

    b) Use a metaphor to describe an urban landscape.

    ....

    c) Use a simile to describe the feeling of embarrassment.

    ....

Q3   Write a descriptive sentence about a busy leisure centre based on each of the following senses.

    a) sight

    ....

    b) sound

    ....

    c) touch

    ....

Section Seven — Writing: Creative Texts

Writing Creatively — Questions

These questions will give you some exam-style practice at writing stories and descriptions.

Q4 Answer the exam-style question below.

> You want to submit a piece of creative writing to be published in your local newspaper. The paper's editor will decide which submissions to publish.
>
> Write a short story that is set in your local area.

Make sure you:
1. <u>Plan</u> how you will structure your story.
2. Use interesting and varied <u>vocabulary</u> to make your story engaging.
3. Use a variety of <u>sentence lengths</u> to make your writing more interesting.

Q5 Answer the exam-style question below.

> You have a pen pal of a similar age to you who lives in another country. In their last letter, they asked you to tell them about any interesting buildings in your area.
>
> Write a letter back to them in which you give a description of an interesting building.

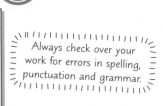
Always check over your work for errors in spelling, punctuation and grammar.

Q6 Answer the exam-style question below.

> You are going to submit a story to an anthology aimed at people who have an interest in travel.
>
> Write a short story suggested by this picture:
>
>

 Make sure your writing is adapted to your audience...

Paper 1, question 5 will tell you who your audience is, so make sure your story or description appeals to that audience. See pages 20-21 for some tips on writing for a particular audience.

Section Eight — Writing: Non-Fiction Texts

Writing Non-Fiction

There are a variety of non-fiction texts you could be asked to write in paper 2, question 5.

Newspaper articles report events and offer opinions

1) Newspaper articles can be written to <u>inform</u>, <u>entertain</u>, <u>argue</u> or <u>advise</u>.

2) Some newspaper articles <u>only</u> report <u>facts</u> about a story or theme.
   They often use an <u>unemotional</u> tone and a <u>formal</u> style. This makes the information seem <u>reliable</u>.

3) Other newspaper articles, called <u>commentaries</u>, offer the <u>writer's viewpoint</u> on a news story or theme.

> Commentaries can also be called <u>columns</u>, <u>editorials</u> or <u>opinion pieces</u>.

4) <u>Commentaries</u> use a <u>personal</u> tone and a <u>conversational</u> style.
   This helps to convey the <u>opinions</u> and <u>personality</u> of the writer.

> *We all need to relax and stop fretting. Nobody's going to bulldoze our green spaces — they'd have to spend 25 years making a planning application first.*

This uses <u>shortened</u> words like 'they'd' to create a conversational style. This makes the writing more <u>entertaining</u> for the reader.

5) Newspaper articles often use <u>layout features</u> to make a text <u>clear</u> and <u>interesting</u> for the reader.

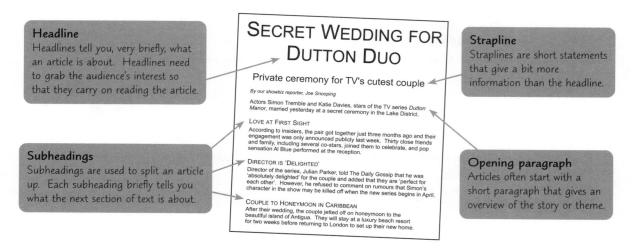

Headline
Headlines tell you, very briefly, what an article is about. Headlines need to grab the audience's interest so that they carry on reading the article.

Strapline
Straplines are short statements that give a bit more information than the headline.

Subheadings
Subheadings are used to split an article up. Each subheading briefly tells you what the next section of text is about.

Opening paragraph
Articles often start with a short paragraph that gives an overview of the story or theme.

SECRET WEDDING FOR DUTTON DUO

Private ceremony for TV's cutest couple

By our showbiz reporter, Joe Snooping

Actors Simon Tremble and Katie Davies, stars of the TV series *Dutton Manor*, married yesterday at a secret ceremony in the Lake District.

LOVE AT FIRST SIGHT
According to insiders, the pair got together just three months ago and their engagement was only announced publicly last week. Thirty close friends and family, including several co-stars, joined them to celebrate, and pop sensation Al Blue performed at the reception.

DIRECTOR IS 'DELIGHTED'
Director of the series, Julian Parker, told The Daily Gossip that he was 'absolutely delighted' for the couple and added that they are 'perfect for each other'. However, he refused to comment on rumours that Simon's character in the show may be killed off when the new series begins in April.

COUPLE TO HONEYMOON IN CARIBBEAN
After their wedding, the couple jetted off on honeymoon to the beautiful island of Antigua. They will stay at a luxury beach resort for two weeks before returning to London to set up their new home.

Leaflets can have varied audiences and purposes

1) Leaflets can have <u>any</u> purpose, but they're often used to <u>advise</u> or <u>persuade</u> an audience.

2) Leaflets need a <u>clear structure</u> to <u>break up</u> information. This could include:

> • a clear title   • bullet points   • subheadings

3) They also use <u>language techniques</u> to grab the reader's attention.

> *Are you searching for a new hobby? If so, why not try learning a new language? It's a fulfilling, exciting and fun way to spend your spare time.*

This leaflet uses a <u>list of three</u> and <u>rhetorical questions</u> to make the text <u>interesting</u> for the reader.

Writing Non-Fiction

Reports and essays inform or advise their audience

1) Reports and essays are texts that go through the arguments <u>for</u> and <u>against</u> something, then come to a conclusion that shows the writer's <u>point of view</u>.

2) Reports and essays should follow a <u>logical structure</u>. They need to have:

> • An <u>introduction</u> that sets up the <u>main theme</u>.
>
> • Well-structured <u>paragraphs</u> going through the arguments <u>for</u> and <u>against</u> something.
>
> • A <u>conclusion</u> that offers <u>your own</u> point of view.

3) They should be written using <u>formal</u> language and have a <u>serious</u> tone.

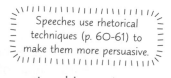
Speeches use rhetorical techniques (p. 60-61) to make them more persuasive.

Speeches need to be dramatic and engaging

1) <u>Speeches</u> are often written to <u>argue</u> or <u>persuade</u>, so they need to have an <u>emotional impact</u>.

2) You can use lots of <u>language techniques</u> to make your writing <u>engaging</u> and <u>persuasive</u>. For example:

> *To me, these accusations are hateful, hurtful and humiliating, and I'm sure you feel the same.* <u>Alliteration</u> and a <u>list of three</u> adjectives make this <u>sound</u> strong and angry. Using the word '<u>you</u>' makes the reader feel <u>involved</u>.

Letters need to start and end correctly

1) The <u>purpose</u> of a letter can be almost anything — it will <u>vary</u> for each letter.

2) The <u>audience</u> of a letter is always a <u>specific</u> person, so you need to <u>adapt</u> your writing to <u>suit</u> that person.

3) If a letter is to someone you <u>don't</u> know well, or to someone in a position of <u>authority</u>, you should:

> • Use <u>formal greetings</u> (e.g. 'Dear Sir/Madam') and <u>sign-offs</u> (e.g. 'Yours sincerely' if you've used their name, 'Yours faithfully' if you haven't).
>
> • Use <u>Standard English</u> and <u>formal language</u>, e.g. you could use phrases like 'In my opinion...' or 'I find this state of affairs...'.

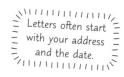
Letters often start with your address and the date.

4) If the letter is to someone you <u>know</u>, or someone who <u>isn't</u> in a position of authority, you should:

> • Start with your reader's <u>name</u>, e.g. 'Dear Jenny', and <u>sign off</u> with 'best wishes' or 'warm regards'.
>
> • Use <u>less formal</u> language, but still write in <u>Standard English</u> (no <u>text speak</u> or <u>slang</u>) and use interesting <u>vocabulary</u>.

KEY SKILL

I'm quite good at writing letters — A, Q, R, Z, F...

As part of your revision, try reading examples of real non-fiction texts. You'll be able to see the kind of language and structure they use, which you can use to help you write a top-notch answer.

Writing Non-Fiction

Adapt your writing to suit the type of text

1) Your writing needs to be <u>appropriate</u> for the type of text you're asked to write. Think about:

> - What <u>tone</u> and <u>style</u> you will need for that <u>type</u> of text.
> - How you can adapt your writing to suit the <u>audience</u>.
> - How you can achieve the <u>purpose</u> of the text.

2) Have a look at the <u>exam-style</u> questions and answers on this page and the next.

3) There's an example of a <u>commentary article</u> from a <u>newspaper</u> on this page, and an example of a <u>speech</u> on the next page.

PAPER 2

| 0 | 5 |

'You will never be able to get the real feel of a place by taking a guided tour. The true heart of any country lies off the beaten track.'

Write a newspaper article in which you explain your point of view on this statement.

Headline
Your headline needs to be short and punchy to interest the reader.

FORGET THE ROAD LESS TRAVELLED
Guided tours are the best way to experience somewhere new.

Strapline
Use a strapline to summarise the article in an interesting way.

Personal tone
Using the pronoun 'we' and conversational language like 'At some point or other' gives this text a <u>personal tone</u>. This creates familiarity with the reader, which helps the writer to share their <u>viewpoint</u> in a friendly way.

At some point or other, we've all been faced with a travel snob: that particular breed of rough-and-tumble traveller who knows all about where to go, what to see and, most importantly, how to see it. The travel snob thinks that guided tours are for the uncultured bores of this planet. The travel snob believes in travel without a destination. And yet, the travel snob will always find time to tell you about a 'hidden gem' that only they can take you to.

You would think someone so educated in the ways of the world would have realised the irony by now — travel snobs are themselves tour guides. The places that they think are 'off the beaten track' are transported, by their own recommendation, right onto 'the beaten track'. They are the one beating the track; they are leading the tourists away from their well-populated honeypot attractions into 'the heart of things'.

In the meantime, guided tours are often run by local people, who will frequently have a real treasure trove of local knowledge. How can a throwaway recommendation from an outsider possibly surpass that? Anybody who wants to see the true heart of a country must be guided by the people who live in it.

Repetition
Repeating 'The travel snob' helps the writer show their <u>point of view</u> — that they disapprove of people who dislike guided tours.

Answer the question
Using some words from the question prompt helps to keep this answer on track.

Rhetorical question
This rhetorical question adds to the <u>conversational style</u> and <u>personal tone</u>. It also helps to <u>persuade</u> the reader to agree with the writer's viewpoint.

Writer's point of view
The writer's <u>viewpoint</u> is clearly stated here, showing that the question is being answered.

Writing Non-Fiction

0 5 'The practice of keeping animals in zoos cannot be allowed to continue. It is inhumane and encourages the use of animals as mere entertainment.'

Write a speech to be delivered at an animal welfare conference, in which you persuade your audience to agree with your point of view on this statement.

Ladies and gentlemen, I have called you here today to defend the practice of keeping animals in captivity. I believe that zoos represent a positive presence in this country.

The view that it is inhumane to keep animals in zoos ignores one of the fundamental reasons why zoos exist. Many species that are kept in captivity are there because they are at risk of extinction without our protection. It would, in fact, be inhumane to leave those animals to be wiped out when we have the ability to prevent such a tragedy.

To say that animals in zoos are used purely for entertainment is also utterly misguided: the vast majority of modern British zoos are focused on educating their visitors as well as entertaining them. To my mind, this aim is worth preserving. It is essential that we give our youngsters an awareness of the world around them. We must impress upon the youth of today the need to protect endangered species and habitats. Zoos can help us to do this. Modern zoos offer extensive opportunities for these kinds of educational experiences: there are interactive exhibitions, talks from conservationists and live question-and-answer forums that will help to educate our young people.

Zoos can help us to protect vulnerable species from extinction. Zoos can help us inspire a generation with the importance of conservation. Zoos can help us by providing a space in which we can work together to build a safer, greener and more ecologically friendly world.

Address the listeners
This speaks directly to the listeners and announces the reason for the speech. This shows the examiner that the <u>purpose</u> and <u>audience</u> have been considered.

Writer's viewpoint
The writer's <u>opinion</u> is clearly stated here, showing that the question is being answered.

Emotive language
'Tragedy' emphasises that it would be devastating if animals were left to become extinct. This makes the reader sympathise with the writer's viewpoint, and <u>persuades</u> them that zoos can be beneficial.

Urgent tone
The word 'must' creates a sense of <u>urgency</u>, making the listeners feel that the speaker's points are important.

Short sentence
The use of a short sentence amongst longer sentences sounds dramatic and forceful, helping to <u>emphasise</u> the point being made.

Repetition
Repeating 'Zoos can help us' emphasises that zoos can be beneficial, <u>persuading</u> the reader to agree.

List of three
This highlights the benefits that zoos can bring in a powerful way, making a <u>persuasive</u> final point.

Chester was ready for his big speech on the importance of daily belly rubs.

© muzon/iStockphoto.com

EXAM TIP

Ladies, gentlemen, and assorted zoo animals...

Paper 2 is called 'Writers' Viewpoints and Perspectives'. So you need to make sure that your own viewpoint comes across when you write your non-fiction text for question 5 in the exam.

Writing Non-Fiction — Questions

Q1   Read the sentences below, then rewrite them so that they're suitable for an opinion piece in a newspaper.

Remember — opinion pieces are generally written in a personal tone.

a) "Doctors have warned of the problems the nation faces if the number of smokers in this country does not decrease."

No-one likes being lectured, but the doctors' warnings are clear — we can't carry on like this.

b) "The government have today announced a policy that will see unsupervised children banned from public places."

....

c) "Temperatures soared across the country this weekend in an unprecedented heat wave."

....

Q2   Read the exam-style question below, then write a suitable opening on the dotted lines.

> "Fast-food chains make it difficult for independent restaurants to make any money. They should be banned."
> Write a newspaper article arguing the case for or against this statement.

Remember to include a headline in your answer.

....

....

....

....

Q3   Read the question below, then write a brief plan to show how you would structure your answer.

> "Space travel is expensive and dangerous. We should stop exploring space."
> Write an essay in which you explain your point of view on this statement.

Introduction: ....

1) ....

2) ....

3) ....

Conclusion: ....

Writing Non-Fiction — Questions

Have a go at these exam-style questions on writing non-fiction texts.

Q4 Read the following extract from a newspaper article.

> ## CRISIS FOR CLASSICAL MUSIC
>
> A report released today by the RBMS (Royal British Music Society) claims that up to 50% of young people in Britain have never listened to a piece of classical music. A further 24% say that they have heard a piece of classical music, but 'would not choose' to listen to the genre.
>
> The report, which was commissioned by the Society in response to a decline in attendance at many live concerts, has provoked concern amongst the musical fraternity, with many claiming that classical music could meet an untimely end if further action is not taken.
>
> Luigi Piccolo, head of the world-renowned Royston Philharmonic Orchestra, said: "Over the next fifty years or so, we're going to become completely irrelevant. It's time to start appealing to a wider audience."

Make it clear what your opinion on the report is.

Write an opinion column to be published alongside this article, in which you explain your point of view on the report.

Q5 Answer the following exam-style question.

> "Pizza is too unhealthy. We should ban it from being served to anyone under the age of eighteen."
>
> Write a speech to be delivered at a national conference of restaurant-owners in which you argue your point of view on this statement.

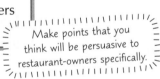
Make points that you think will be persuasive to restaurant-owners specifically.

Q6 Answer the exam-style question below.

> 'Keeping fit as a student is too hard. Gym memberships and exercise equipment are too expensive for young people, and students don't have time to exercise.'
>
> Write the text for a leaflet in which you advise students about how to keep fit.

Plan your answer before you start writing...

Always do a plan for the writing questions in both papers — it will help you to organise your ideas into an effective structure. Have a look at page 20 for some tips on how to plan your answers.

Section Nine — Practice Exams

Paper 1 — Questions

This section has two practice exam papers in it. They're similar to the two exams you'll take for your AQA GCSE in English Language. To start with, have a look at this practice exam for paper 1.

Try answering these questions as if you were in a real exam — give yourself 1 hour 45 minutes to read through the source and answer all five questions.

The source for these questions is on page 84.

Section A — Reading

You should spend about 15 minutes reading the source and all the questions.

*Then you should spend about 45 minutes answering **all** the questions in this section.*

0 1   Read again lines 12 to 19 of the source.

List **four** things from this part of the text about the baby.

[4 marks]

0 2   Look in detail at lines 1 to 11 of the source.

How does the writer use language here to describe Mabel's life in Alaska?

You could include the writer's choice of:

- words and phrases
- language features and techniques
- sentence forms.

[8 marks]

0 3   You now need to think about the **whole** of the **source**.

This text is from the opening of a novel.

How has the writer structured the text to interest you as a reader?

You could write about:

- the time that the writer focuses on at the beginning
- how and why the writer changes the time she is writing about as the extract develops
- any other structural features that interest you.

The text's structure didn't seem to have interested the audience very much at all.

[8 marks]

Paper 1 — Questions

0 4   Focus this part of your answer on the last part of the source, **from line 20 to the end**.

A student, having read this section of the text, said: "The writer makes it really clear how Mabel is feeling. It makes me feel the emotions she's feeling too."

To what extent do you agree?

In your response, you could:

- write about your own feelings on reading the passage

- evaluate how the writer created those feelings

- support your opinions with quotations from the text.

[20 marks]

Section B — Writing

You should spend about 45 minutes answering the question in this section.
You are advised to plan your answer.
Write using full sentences.

0 5   You are going to enter a creative writing competition.

Your entry will be judged by a panel of people of your own age.

Either:

Write a description suggested by this picture:

© wingmar/iStockphoto.com

Or:

Write the opening part of a story that is set in a cold place in winter.

(24 marks for content and organisation
16 marks for technical accuracy)

[40 marks]

Paper 1 — Exam Source

Here's the text to go with the questions on pages 82-83. It's an extract from the opening of *The Snow Child* by Eowyn Ivey, a novel which was published in 2012, but is set in 1920. In the novel, a woman named Mabel and her husband, Jack, have moved to the cold, remote Alaskan wilderness to start a new life.

Wolverine River, Alaska, 1920

Mabel had known there would be silence. That was the point, after all. No infants cooing or wailing. No neighbor children playfully hollering down the lane. No pad of small feet on wooden stairs worn smooth by generations, or clackety-clack of toys along the kitchen floor. All those sounds of her failure and regret would be left behind, and in their place there would be silence.

5   She had imagined that in the Alaska wilderness silence would be peaceful, like snow falling at night, air filled with promise but no sound, but that was not what she found. Instead, when she swept the plank floor, the broom bristles scritched like some sharp-toothed shrew nibbling at her heart. When she washed the dishes, plates and bowls clattered as if they were breaking to pieces. The only sound not of her making was a sudden 'caw, cawww' from outside. Mabel wrung dishwater from a rag and looked out the kitchen

10   window in time to see a raven flapping its way from one leafless birch tree to another. No children chasing each other through autumn leaves, calling each other's names. Not even a solitary child on a swing.

❊

There had been the one. A tiny thing, born still and silent. Ten years past, but even now she found herself returning to the birth to touch Jack's arm, stop him, reach out. She should have. She should have cupped the baby's head in the palm of her hand and snipped a few of its tiny hairs to keep in a locket at her throat.

15   She should have looked into its small face and known if it was a boy or a girl, and then stood beside Jack as he buried it in the Pennsylvania winter ground. She should have marked its grave. She should have allowed herself that grief.

It was a child, after all, although it looked more like a fairy changeling. Pinched face, tiny jaw, ears that came to narrow points; that much she had seen and wept over because she knew she could have loved it still.

❊

20   Mabel was too long at the window. The raven had since flown away above the treetops. The sun had slipped behind a mountain, and the light had fallen flat. The branches were bare, the grass yellowed gray. Not a single snowflake. It was as if everything fine and glittering had been ground from the world and swept away as dust.

November was here, and it frightened her because she knew what it brought — cold upon the valley

25   like a coming death, glacial wind through the cracks between the cabin logs. But most of all, darkness. Darkness so complete even the pale-lit hours would be choked.

She entered last winter blind, not knowing what to expect in this new, hard land. Now she knew. By December, the sun would rise just before noon and skirt the mountaintops for a few hours of twilight before sinking again. Mabel would move in and out of sleep as she sat in a chair beside the woodstove. She

30   would not pick up any of her favorite books; the pages would be lifeless. She would not draw; what would there be to capture in her sketchbook? Dull skies, shadowy corners. It would become harder and harder to leave the warm bed each morning. She would stumble about in a walking sleep, scrape together meals and drape wet laundry around the cabin. Jack would struggle to keep the animals alive. The days would run together, winter's stranglehold tightening.

35   All her life she had believed in something more, in the mystery that shape-shifted at the edge of her senses. It was the flutter of moth wings on glass and the promise of river nymphs in the dappled creek beds. It was the smell of oak trees on the summer evening she fell in love, and the way dawn threw itself across the cow pond and turned the water to light.

Mabel could not remember the last time she caught such a flicker.

Paper 2 — Questions

This practice exam is for paper 2.

Try to answer these questions as you would in a real exam — give yourself
1 hour 45 minutes to read through the sources and answer all five questions.

The sources to go with these questions are on pages 87-88.

Section A — Reading

*You should spend about 15 minutes reading
the sources and all the questions.*

*Then you should spend about 45 minutes
answering **all** the questions in this section.*

0 1   Read the first part of **source A**, from lines 1 to 17.

Choose **four** statements below which are **TRUE**.

- Shade the boxes of the ones that you think are true

- Choose a maximum of four statements.

A   Lisa made her first batches of soup with her parents.   ☐

B   Lisa wasn't initially excited about making and selling soup.   ☐

C   Lisa's parents liked the first sample of soup she made them try.   ☐

D   Lisa's aunt didn't like throwing food away.   ☐

E   Lisa's parents thought the business was a great idea from the start.   ☐

F   People were surprised by Lisa working at such a young age.   ☐

G   Lisa's dad wasn't very good at negotiating with farmers.   ☐

H   Lisa chose working on her business over spending time with friends.   ☐

[4 marks]

0 2   You need to refer to **source A** and the **whole of source B** for this question:

Use details from **both** sources. Write a summary of the differences between
Lisa Goodwin's parents and the parents of the Victorian street sellers.

[8 marks]

Paper 2 — Questions

0 3 You now need to refer **only** to **source B**, the interview with the flower seller.

How does the flower seller use language to appeal to the reader's emotions?

[12 marks]

0 4 For this question, you need to refer to the **whole of source A** together with **source B**, the interview with the nut seller.

Compare how Lisa Goodwin and the nut seller convey their different attitudes to work and childhood.

In your answer, you should:

- compare their different attitudes

- compare the methods they use to convey their attitudes

- support your ideas with quotations from both texts.

[16 marks]

Section B — Writing

You should spend about 45 minutes answering the question in this section.
You are advised to plan your answer.
Write using full sentences.

0 5 "More children should get a job before the age of sixteen. Part-time work would teach children valuable skills that they don't learn in school."

Write an article for a newspaper in which you argue the case for or against this statement.

(24 marks for content and organisation
16 marks for technical accuracy)

[40 marks]

Sooner or later, Lisa was going to realise she needed a smaller spoon.

Paper 2 — Exam Source A

Here is exam source A, to go with the questions on pages 85-86. It's a biographical article written by a young entrepreneur (a person who starts up a business) for a newspaper in the 1990s.

Setting up SouperStar — From Soup Pan to Soup Stand

Lisa Goodwin recalls how she set up her first business at the age of eight.

When I first told my parents that I wanted to sell soup, I must have been about eight years old — like most sensible parents, they thought I was joking. That weekend, I'd been at my aunt's house helping her harvest vegetables from her garden. It had been a bumper year, and we'd been staggering back and forth, shifting armfuls of all sorts of things into to the house. With my aunt, not a single thing could
5 go to waste, so we set about making soup. Gallons of the stuff. We were surrounded by steaming and bubbling pots and pans, and the air was thick with scents of leek and potato, carrot and coriander and spicy butternut squash. Anyway, when my parents didn't take me seriously, I went straight to the fridge to dig out one of the soups my aunt and I had made — it was cream of mushroom, I think — and they absolutely lapped it up. "See!" I said, smiling. So it was then that SouperStar was born.

10 From day one I couldn't wait to get stuck in. My parents would dutifully help me select produce, whizz up batches of soup and drive me here, there and everywhere so that I could set up shop. I would go to school fairs, farmers' markets — anywhere that would have me. Dad was my champion haggler. He'd barter with local farmers to get crates of carrots or potatoes at rock-bottom prices. If he could get anything for free, well, that was even better! I think a lot of people were bemused by the sight of this
15 young kid, buying produce and selling soup, and my parents put up with it because they thought that I would grow out of it at some stage. While other kids my age were glued to the TV or playing in the park, I was peeling vegetables and frying croutons.

I begged and pleaded with my parents to let me be home-schooled, as I wanted to dedicate more time to the business, but they insisted I should have a "normal" childhood, and fill my head with "necessary" stuff
20 like formulae and equations. A few years later, and I was sitting my O levels* — but instead of panicking over revision, I was, of course, dreaming up new recipes. With all my exams passed and done with, I wanted to press on and really dedicate myself to SouperStar. I think at this point my parents genuinely realised how determined I was, and they began to take it a lot more seriously too.

I struck upon the idea of selling soup at our local train station during the winter months — there was a
25 constant stream of customers all in desperate need of something that would warm up their hands and fill their bellies. Before long, I was hiring extra staff in order to open up soup stands in other nearby train stations and Mum was coming up with advertising slogans and snazzy package designs (her years of marketing experience came in pretty handy here). As the business grew and grew, Mum and Dad couldn't keep up with all the support I needed, so it made sense for them to get even more involved.
30 Mum reduced her hours at work and Dad quit his job entirely. Fast-forward to today, and I'm the managing director of one the most successful food companies in the area.

Of course, financially, it's worked out well for us (thanks must go to my parents for the initial investment, not to mention being old enough to buy the wine for my French onion soup!), but for me it was never the dream of becoming a millionaire that got me started or even kept me going. It was the passion for
35 building a great business based on great food — and that remains at the heart of SouperStar today.

Glossary
* O levels — the qualifications that came before GCSEs, with examinations taken at the age of 16.

Paper 2 — Exam Source B

This is exam source B, to go with the questions on pages 85-86. It's two interviews from the 1840s, conducted with children who work as street sellers. These articles, along with many others, were published in a newspaper to highlight the problem of poverty in London.

The first interview is with a young girl who sells flowers, and is an orphan.

"Mother has been dead just a year this month; she took cold at the washing and it went to her chest; she was only bad a fortnight; she suffered great pain, and, poor thing, she used to fret dreadful, as she lay ill, about me, for she knew she was going to leave me. She used to plan how I was to do when she was gone. She made me promise to try to get a place and keep from the streets if I could, for she seemed
5   to dread them so much. When she was gone I was left in the world without a friend. I am quite alone, I have no relation at all, not a soul belonging to me. For three months I went about looking for a place, as long as my money lasted, for mother told me to sell our furniture to keep me and get me clothes. I could have got a place, but nobody would have me without a character*, and I knew nobody to give me one. I tried very hard to get one, indeed I did; for I thought of all mother had said to me about going into the
10 streets. At last, when my money was just gone, I met a young woman in the street, and I asked her to tell me where I could get a lodging. She told me to come with her, she would show me a respectable lodging-house for women and girls. I went, and I have been there ever since. The women in the house advised me to take to flower-selling, as I could get nothing else to do. One of the young women took me to market with her, and showed me how to bargain with the salesman for my flowers. At first, when I went out to
15 sell, I felt so ashamed I could not ask anybody to buy of me; and many times went back at night with all my stock, without selling one bunch. The woman at the lodging house is very good to me; when I have a bad day she will let my lodging go until I can pay her. She is very kind, indeed, for she knows I am alone. What I shall do in the winter I don't know. In the cold weather last year, when I could get no flowers, I was forced to live on my clothes, I have none left now but what I have on. What I shall do I don't know — I
20 can't bear to think on it."

The second interview is with a young girl who sells nuts.

"It's in the winter, sir, when things are far worst with us. Father can make very little then — but I don't know what he earns exactly at any time — and though mother has more work then, there's fire and candle to pay for. We were very badly off last winter, and worse, I think, the winter before. Father sometimes came home and had made nothing, and if mother had no work in hand we went to bed to save fire and
25 candle, if it was ever so soon. Father would die afore he would let mother take as much as a loaf from the parish. I was sent out to sell nuts first: 'If it's only 1d.** you make,' mother said, 'it's a good piece of bread.' I didn't mind being sent out. I knew children that sold things in the streets. Perhaps I liked it better than staying at home without a fire and with nothing to do, and if I went out I saw other children busy. No, I wasn't a bit frightened when I first started, not a bit. Some children — but they was such little
30 things — said: 'O, Liz, I wish I was you.' I had twelve ha'porths*** and sold them all. I don't know what it made; 2d. most likely. I didn't crack a single nut myself. I was fond of them then, but I don't care for them now. I could do better if I went into public-houses, but I'm only let go to Mr. Smith's, because he knows father, and Mrs. Smith and him recommends me. I have sold nuts and oranges to soldiers. I was once in a great crowd, and was getting crushed, and there was a very tall soldier close by me, and he lifted me,
35 basket and all, right up to his shoulder, and carried me clean out of the crowd. He had stripes on his arm. 'I shouldn't like you to be in such a trade,' says he, 'if you was my child.' He didn't say why he wouldn't like it. Perhaps because it was beginning to rain. Yes, we are far better off now. Father makes money. I don't go out in bad weather in the summer; in the winter, though, I must. I don't know what I shall be when I grow up. I can read a little. I've been to church five or six times in my life. I should go oftener and
40 so would mother, if we had clothes."

Glossary
* a character — a reference
** d. — pence
*** ha'porths — half-pennys' worth

Glossary

adjective	A word that <u>describes</u> a noun or a pronoun, e.g. heavy, kind, unusual.
adverb	A word that gives <u>extra information</u> about a <u>verb</u>, e.g. carefully, rarely, tightly.
alliteration	When words that are <u>close together</u> start with the <u>same sound</u>. E.g. "the <u>b</u>eat of the <u>b</u>and".
analogy	A <u>comparison</u> to show how one thing is <u>similar</u> to another, which makes it easier to <u>understand</u> or more <u>memorable</u>. E.g. "watching cricket is about as exciting as watching paint dry."
audience	The <u>person</u> or <u>group of people</u> that read or listen to a text.
cliffhanger	An <u>ending</u> to a text that leaves the reader wondering what will happen <u>next</u>.
command	A sentence that <u>tells</u> the reader to do something. It might also be called an <u>order</u>.
commentary (newspaper article)	A type of newspaper article that expresses the <u>opinions</u> of the writer on a theme or news event. Also called a <u>column</u> or <u>opinion piece</u>.
contraction	The <u>shortened</u> form of a word or group of words, normally using an <u>apostrophe</u>. E.g. 'we're' is a contraction of 'we are'.
conversational style	A style of writing that uses <u>informal</u> language that would normally be used in <u>spoken</u> conversation.
cumulative effect	When types of words or phrases are <u>repeated</u>, leading to a <u>build-up</u> of their effects.
direct address	When a writer talks <u>straight to the reader</u>, e.g. "you might recall..."
double negative	A phrase that <u>incorrectly</u> expresses a <u>negative idea</u> by using <u>two</u> negative words or phrases, e.g. "I <u>don't</u> want <u>no</u> trouble."
emotive language	Language that has an <u>emotional</u> effect on the reader.
empathy	The ability to <u>imagine</u> and <u>understand</u> someone else's <u>feelings</u> or <u>experiences</u>.
exclamation	A sentence that shows strong <u>emotions</u>, usually ending with an <u>exclamation mark</u>.
explicit information	Information that's <u>directly stated</u> in a text.
fiction	Writing that recounts events that are <u>not factual</u>, e.g. stories.
flashback	A writing technique where the scene shifts from the <u>present</u> to an event in the <u>past</u>.
form	The <u>type</u> of text, e.g. a letter, a speech or a newspaper article.

Glossary

hyperbole	When <u>exaggeration</u> is used to have an <u>effect</u> on the reader, e.g. "The vase smashed into a million tiny pieces."
imagery	Language techniques that create a <u>picture in your mind</u>, e.g. metaphors and similes.
impersonal tone	A tone of writing that doesn't reveal much about the writer's <u>emotions</u> or <u>personality</u>.
implicit information	Information that's hinted at <u>without</u> being said outright.
inference	A <u>conclusion</u> reached about something, based on <u>evidence</u>. E.g. from the sentence "Yasmin wrinkled her nose at the peas", you could <u>infer</u> that Yasmin doesn't like peas.
irony	Saying one thing but meaning the <u>opposite</u>. E.g. "What a great idea of mine to go for a nice long walk on the rainiest day of the year."
journalistic style	A <u>balanced</u> way of reporting news that shows opinions on <u>both</u> sides of an argument.
language	The <u>choice of words</u> and <u>phrases</u> used.
linear structure	Writing that tells the events of a story in <u>time</u> order.
list of three	Using <u>three</u> words (often adjectives) or phrases together to create <u>emphasis</u>.
metaphor	A way of <u>describing</u> something by saying that it <u>is</u> something else, to create a vivid image. E.g. "His eyes were deep blue pools."
narrative	Writing that tells a <u>story</u> or describes an <u>experience</u>.
narrator	The <u>voice</u> or <u>character</u> speaking the words of the narrative.
non-fiction	Writing that is about <u>real-life</u> events. E.g. newspaper articles, diary entries, letters.
non-linear structure	Writing that tells the events of a story <u>out of time order</u>.
noun	A <u>naming</u> word that refers to a <u>person</u>, <u>thing</u>, <u>place</u> or <u>idea</u>, e.g. Alex, soup, Germany, freedom.
onomatopoeia	A word that <u>imitates</u> the sound it describes as you say it, e.g. 'whisper'.
paraphrase	Describing or rephrasing something in a text <u>without</u> including a direct quote.
personal tone	A tone of writing that gives a clear sense of the writer's <u>emotions</u> or <u>personality</u>.
personification	Describing something as if it's a <u>person</u>. E.g. "The sea growled hungrily."
phrase	A <u>group</u> of words, usually <u>without</u> a <u>verb</u>. E.g. "Time and time again".
plot twist	An <u>unexpected</u> event in a story which <u>surprises</u> or <u>shocks</u> the reader.

Glossary

Glossary

possessive pronoun	A <u>pronoun</u> such as 'yours' or 'mine' that tells you who something <u>belongs</u> to.
pronoun	A word that can <u>take the place</u> of a noun in a sentence, e.g. 'he', 'she', 'it'.
purpose	The <u>reason</u> someone writes a text. E.g. to persuade, to argue, to advise, to inform.
quotation	Text that is taken <u>directly</u> from a piece of writing, written using <u>quotation marks</u> (" ").
repetition	The technique of <u>repeating</u> words or phrases for effect.
rhetoric	The use of <u>language</u> techniques (e.g. repetition or hyperbole) to achieve a persuasive <u>effect</u>.
rhetorical question	A question that <u>doesn't need an answer</u>, but is used to <u>persuade</u> the reader. E.g. "Why do we do this to ourselves?"
simile	A way of describing something by <u>comparing</u> it to something else, usually by using the words 'like' or 'as'. E.g. "He was as pale as the moon."
slang	Words or phrases that are <u>informal</u>, and often specific to one <u>age</u> group or <u>social</u> group.
Standard English	English that is considered to be <u>correct</u> because it uses formal, standardised features of <u>spelling</u> and <u>grammar</u>.
statement	A type of sentence that is used to deliver <u>information</u>.
strapline	A <u>short statement</u> at the <u>start</u> of a newspaper article that <u>expands</u> on the headline.
structure	The <u>order</u> and <u>arrangement</u> of ideas in a text. E.g. how the text begins, develops and ends.
style	The <u>way</u> in which a text is <u>written</u>, including the type of language, sentence forms and structure used.
summary	A short account of a lot of <u>information</u>, rewritten using <u>your own</u> words.
technical terms	<u>Special words</u> used when studying English Language to describe things like language <u>techniques</u>, e.g. 'onomatopoeia' or 'metaphor'.
tense	A verb's <u>tense</u> tells you whether something is happening in the <u>past</u>, <u>present</u> or <u>future</u>, e.g. "I <u>had</u> a bath" = past tense, "I <u>will have</u> a bath" = future tense.
tone	The <u>mood</u> or <u>feeling</u> of a piece of writing, e.g. happy, sad, serious, light-hearted.
verb	A <u>doing</u> or <u>being</u> word, e.g. dig, breathe, are, is.
viewpoint	The <u>attitude</u> and <u>beliefs</u> that a writer is trying to convey.

Index